LORR

90 DAYS TO LEARNING THE TAROT

NO MEMORIZATION REQUIRED!

KING OF PENTAC

OF PENTACLES

Schiffer Publishing Ltd

4880 Lower Valley Road • Atglen, PA 19310

Type set in Bodoni Std/Book Antiqua

ISBN: 978-0-7643-4774-0
Printed in China

Schiffer Books are available at special discounts for bulk purchases for sales promotions or premiums. Special editions, including personalized covers, corporate imprints, and excerpts can be created in large quantities for special needs. For more information contact the publisher:

Published by Schiffer Publishing, Ltd.
4880 Lower Valley Road
Atglen, PA 19310
Phone: (610) 593-1777; Fax: (610) 593-2002
E-mail: Info@schifferbooks.com

For the largest selection of fine reference books on this and related subjects, please visit our website at **www.schifferbooks.com.**

We are always looking for people to write books on new and related subjects. If you have an idea for a book, please contact us at proposals@schifferbooks.com.

This book may be purchased from the publisher. Please try your bookstore first. You may write for a free catalog.

Cover and inside card images: *The Gilded Tarot* © 2004 Ciro Marchetti; Lewellyn Publications, 2143 Woodbury, MN 55125. Used by permission.

Other photo credits: Courtesy Elizabeth Galecke Photography and David Blevins.

EPIGRAM

"What we call 'I'
is just a swinging door
that moves
when we inhale
and when we exhale."

—Shunryu Suzuki
Zen Mind, Beginner's Mind

DEDICATION

For all of you who I have met, am meeting,
or have yet to meet: Thank you for being my teacher.

Acknowledgments

For my introduction to really learning the Tarot and giving readings to others, I am eternally grateful to my first mentor Carol Miriam.

Alisha Olivier Park, thanks for being the first person to tell me that this book needed to be written.

Lencsi Angel, thank you for ALWAYS being my cheerleader. I love you sweet soul sister!

Thank you to all of my wonderful friends (Venus, Rachel, Laxmi, Joan, Erica, Parrish, Phoebe, Cheryl, Guenevere, Karen, Amanda, the Sensibilities Ladies and Chris) and clients. You have taught me so much.

I am grateful to Trisha and Tom Kelly and the Soul of Yoga Community in Encinitas, California, for the memories of unconditional love that I return to in my mind for sustenance again and again as I move forward with my life on the East Coast.

Thank you Davidji for believing in me and being the first person to challenge me to stretch my edges and support my dreams while I was working at The Chopra Center.

Props to Malaprops in Asheville, North Carolina, for your coffee and free Wi-Fi that I totally enjoyed while writing this book.

Thank you Elizabeth Galecke for your amazing photographs and Antoinette Villamil for your editing prowess. Both of you ladies made the final stages of my manuscript preparation seamless and fun!

Thank you Bryan at Patanjali's Place for reminding me of commitment to my dreams.

Thanks to my niece, Betsy Gifford, for being a living example of creativity and my nephew, Justin Gifford, for being a reminder of remaining a quiet observer and complete jokester. Both of you consistently bring a smile to my face. I love being part of your lives.

Thank you Ciro Marcetti; your deck, *The Gilded Tarot*, brings joy to my life and my life's work each and every day.

My gratitude overflows for Dinah Roseberry and the staff at Schiffer Publishing for helping to fulfill a lifelong dream of becoming a published author

And finally, much love and thanks to one of my longest standing friends and spiritual brother, Jesus Benitez. Thank God you were and continue to be at the other end of the phone offering encouragement as I bumble my way through this process called life. LYLT!

Contents

PREFACE

Reading the Tarot is my passion. It offers me the opportunity to be a direct connection for The Divine as I support others. It feeds my soul. But here's my confession: I am just like you.

I don't always wake up excited to start my day or with a serene and beneficent smile. Some mornings I want to stay in bed, burrowed underneath the covers and not deal with the world. On those mornings, I allow myself to wallow for 5-30 minutes before I get up, stretch, put my yoga clothes on, make my bed (so I won't be tempted to crawl back in), and get on my yoga mat to begin my daily practice.

This morning, as I finished my practice and was relaxing in Savasana, I was grateful that I 'd brought my grumpy self to the mat. I moved to my meditation cushion and settled in, allowing my mind to run amuck as it sometimes likes to do. I then reminded myself that this was called "meditation practice" for a reason. I did not reach Samadhi today, but I did soften some of my edges a bit more.

After meditating, I got up and went to the door, thinking a walk outside might be nice. I opened the door and quickly closed it. It was a cold, gray autumn day and I did not want any part if it. So what did I do? I purposely made myself go out and walk anyways. Yes, there are times I want to withdraw and make the comfortable choice. That is when I need to push past the initial resistance and making a different choice. I am happy that I made a different choice this morning, because, that walk reminded me to slow down and breathe. As I walked, I began to notice the crispness of the air on my cheeks and the crunching of the dried leaves as the squirrels skittered about in the woods surrounding me. I walked by a man who gave me a huge smile and said, "Good morning." He was with his dog. As I glanced at the dog, I couldn't help but laugh out loud at how gleeful the dog was to be out for a walk. Joy was coming off her in waves and I swear she had a huge grin. As I rounded the corner, there was a very regal-looking boxer standing on the side of a hill. He was slowly and serenely surveying his world. As he met my eyes, he held them for a few moments, and then I swear he nodded slightly at me before he continued looking around.

It was then that the "aha moment" happened. Everything I was noticing around me was playing out within me. The cold and gray day had mirrored my initial reaction upon waking. The yoga practice and meditation helped to start to move it. All of the parts of my walk that I observed were within me: the grumpy, the lazy, the disciplined, the agitated, the industrious, the joyful, the observant, and the peaceful.

Without my spiritual practices, I would not have noticed anything on my walk and would have remained in my head wishing I were still in bed. It was another affirmation of the importance of starting my day with my practices.

This book offers you the opportunity to begin or continue your own practices while moving through your life in moments of comfort and discomfort. It provides you with many experiences of connecting to your intuition and The Divine within you. We are the same, you and me, so come walk with me and know that even if I am not there, you are never alone, because God is always there with you.

INTRODUCTION

Why Tarot?

My grandfather played a key role during my childhood. I was ten when my parents divorced, and my mother's father stepped in to help. He quickly became the main male influence in my life, and was an equal mixture of Yoda and Archie Bunker wrapped in a brown cardigan sweater. I spent my summers at his house by the lake. We did not have a car, so he was the person I called when I needed a ride to a friend's house, to school, or to the store. As much as he groused, I knew he secretly enjoyed being there for me. In his own way, he paid my allowance: twice a month, he picked me up and paid me to "clean" his house. As a typical teenager, I spent more time on the phone with friends and reading romance novels than actually cleaning. He would often complain about my behavior, but he was always there to pick me up.

His death hit me pretty hard, especially because it was the first death that I had experienced. The concept of never being able to talk to him or hear his voice again was difficult for me to accept. The man who I knew I could always turn to was now gone. The summer after he died, I attended my first Psychic Fair with a friend. The man who gave my reading said that there was a spirit around me; he described my grandfather in exacting detail, down to his brown cardigan sweater and his deafness in one ear.

That reading filled me with hope and gave me a connection to the grandfather I so desperately missed. I was comforted and, for the first time, saw that a relationship could exist past the grave. I began to see the metaphysical world as a bridge to my grandfather. Later that week, I purchased my first deck of Tarot cards.

In the beginning, I kept the knowledge of owning a deck to myself. I occasionally brought the deck out to give myself a reading when I was in need of advice or missing my grandfather. A few years later, while visiting my friend, Trish, for the weekend in Rochester, New York, I received my first professional Tarot card reading.

I was filled with excitement and nervousness as we loaded into the car and headed for my reading at The Village Gate. Carol, the Tarot card reader, laid out the cards and, as she began to read, I was enthralled. She saw a story unfold through each card she placed on the table. As she turned cards over, she paused and told me that I too had the ability to do what she did.

After she finished my reading, Carol picked up the deck, handed it to me and encouraged me to read the cards for her. As I was an "in the closet" reader, I was nervous because I was accustomed to looking in a book to ascertain the meaning for each card. She was asking me to read the cards without any back up! I was so afraid to be wrong, but because she was holding a space filled with unconditional acceptance, I gave it a try. We sat there for the rest of the afternoon as she turned potential clients away and shared her gifts with me. I left The Village Gate with a new friend and mentor. Within six months, I moved to Rochester and, under her guidance, joined The Rochester Psychic Center as their youngest member.

The Tarot and the stories told within the cards are, in my mind, magical. The fact that seventy-eight cards reveal a different story for each person who receives a reading just blows my mind. Even if the same cards were to show up for two different people, chances are the stories would also be different. The cards are the tools I use to tap into my intuition, and through this action, I hear the quiet voice of something greater, a voice filled with love and divinity. I have come to understand that, through using the Tarot, I have the opportunity to offer similar hope and connection to others.

My dream is to provide the tools so that you, too, can tap into your own intuition and hear that quiet voice, which has always been and will always be with you. This book is dedicated to that purpose and to the wonderful teachers I have met along the way.

The book is broken down into ninety daily lessons, each of which contains questions to answer, ideas to consider, or activities in which to take part.

My goal is to keep the instructions simple and reawaken the intuitive voice within you, eliminating the need for you to memorize seventy-eight different cards. As such, this journey is a spiritual one.

There are three sections within this book:

1. Getting to Know Yourself (*Days 1 through 14*)

2. Getting to Know Your Cards (*Days 15 through 75*)

3. Sharing the Messages You Receive (*Days 76 through 90*)

Through this process, you will become confident in your ability to connect to your intuition. Whether you are interested in reading the Tarot for yourself, others, or both, this journey is one that you will find to be supportive.

What started out as a connection to my grandfather transformed into an even bigger connection: a connection with my God source whose unconditional love includes my grandfather's love many times over.

By choosing to embark on this path, you have started the process to create more clarity in your life through the simplicity of these methods, as well as a connection to something higher.

Let your journey through the Tarot begin...

Choosing Your Deck

The first step on this journey is to find the right Tarot deck. Choose one that you feel drawn to. If you do not currently have a deck, schedule some time to go to a local bookstore and peruse the selection.

There are many beautiful Tarot decks available. When you choose a deck, always trust your intuition. See which deck calls to you. For example, I am drawn to colorful decks that tell a story. I also like decks that depict friendly faces and warm eyes. I veer towards and tend to recommend using a deck wherein each card tells a story. My current deck of choice is *The Gilded Tarot*, and its images will be used throughout this book.

Once you have a deck in your possession, answer the following questions:

1. What drew you to this deck?
   (Was it the colors? The images? The theme?)

2. Did you chose it, or was it a gift?
   (The answer does not matter, as long as you feel connected to your divination tool. It is through this tool that you will open up a channel of communication with the Divine.)

3. Are you planning to use it as a tool of self-discovery?
   To help others? Or both?

As you connect with your deck on Days 15 through 75, you will explore the images, symbols, and colors on each card as you continue to notice what makes your deck unique. Becoming acquainted with your deck is essential, as it is your trusted companion on this new journey.

A Brief (Really Brief) Bit of History Before We Start

Have you ever played Solitaire, Go Fish, or Gin Rummy? If you have, then you are familiar with a deck of playing cards, which actually originated from the Tarot deck. Of course, there are a few differences. A deck of playing cards does not have "Pages," and the "Knights" are now "Jacks." Sometimes I wonder if the "Joker" card was meant to symbolize the "Fool"...

The history of the Tarot is surrounded by many different theories. I encourage you to do your own research on the topic. Different speculations aside, one thing remains consistent: the Tarot is filled with beautiful imagery and diverse symbols.

As humans, we associate and relate meanings to symbols, which can be used to tell a story. Through interpreting these symbols, we can gain an understanding of the past, present, or future of a situation. When giving a reading, we can use symbols on the Tarot cards to open the door to allow a story to unfold. This story then becomes the vehicle for "confirmation" or a "reality check" for the person who receives the reading. That same person can choose whether or not to rewrite a particular chapter within the story of her/his life. The cards are a vehicle to connect to a higher source and can be used to communicate one's higher purpose.

In order to begin this journey and have an empowering experience, as well to gain an understanding of the cards, it is important to get to know and understand yourself first. Section One, which covers Days 1 through 14, will build the foundation of your journey. A strong foundation is the key to understanding how to rewrite your story, as well as a way to facilitate space so that your clients can rewrite theirs.

SECTION ONE

Getting to Know Yourself

DAY 1

Balanced or Burned Out?

Ironically, the most unbalanced period in my life was the time in which I worked for a renowned wellness center. This center is internationally known and hundreds of people visit each month, attending programs that incorporate Ayurvedic massage, meditation, and other tools to bring greater balance into their lives. The transformations I witnessed while working there were truly amazing.

I was so busy helping others to find balance in their own lives that I forgot to make time for my own. My workdays consisted of the following: arriving at 7:30 each morning and leaving at 7:30 each evening on weekdays, with a slightly modified schedule from 8 a.m. to 6 p.m. on the weekends. I provided oversight of the spa and therapists, performed the Ayurvedic treatments, and also taught classes, and engaged in one-on-one interactions with the guests. During my last year at the center, I had a handful of days off with only two "complete" days off (Thanksgiving and Christmas). In all fairness, I am not pointing the finger at anyone. Rather, I did not know how to set boundaries for my own well-being. I was lost in the world of trying to be perfect and striving to make everyone happy. (Anyone in management can understand the absurdity of this.) During my last few months at this job, I would awake each night from a sound sleep with anxiety attacks because I had to go back to work in just a few hours.

I finally left this job because I was completely burned out. How could I continue to promote a balanced mind, body, and spirit when I had no sense of personal balance? I was an exhausted workaholic, and I had to leave. After I left that job, it took me a year and a half of incorporating the tools that I had taught to others before my body finally felt rested.

In retrospect, I realize that I had to travel this path to gain an experiential understanding of the importance of balance in my life. Once I had this, I was even more passionate to help facilitate this knowledge for others. I finally learned to walk my talk.

Reading the Tarot is a "healing art," but do not mistake this "healing art" as one-sided. To truly be involved in this occupation, it is important to be on your own path to wholeness as well. This path includes being both selfless and selfish, being of service to others, and taking the needed time to nourish your own self.

Creating a balance between being in your heart, mind, and body is essential to your intuitive practice: the clearer the vessel, the clearer the messages. Taking an HONEST look at your current habits is needed to create a smooth transformation. When you assess how you feed your body, mind, and spirit, you can create your own opportunities for growth and change.

To start this process take a moment

and HONESTLY answer the questions below.

1. How many hours of sleep do you need each night to operate optimally?

2. How many hours do you sleep on an average night?

3. On a scale from one to ten, how rested do you feel today? (One being not at all rested and in need of a week of sleep and ten being completely rested and raring to go.)

4. On that same scale, how rested would you say that you feel on an ongoing basis?

5. What daily spiritual practices do you currently have in place? Some examples include meditation, journaling or prayer.

6. **What physical/exercise practices do you participate in?**

7. **How often do you participate in the practices you mentioned in question six?**

8. **How would you describe your digestion?** (Sluggish, moderate, excellent)

9. **Write down everything that you have had to eat and drink in the past three days.** (Use blank pages provided at the back of the book.)

When I have others answer question nine, I always hear, "This is not how I typically eat!" Guess what? It probably is. The point is to create awareness around your current habits, but not judge them.

Good rest, a daily spiritual practice, a regular exercise or movement practice (such as yoga), and good nutrition are essential for your vitality. The more vital and energized you are, the more receptive you will be to that quiet voice of intuition.

What changes are you willing to make

for the next ninety days?

DAY 2

Just Breathe

As a massage therapist, I have had the pleasure of working on thousands of bodies over the years. One of the most common areas on which I am asked to work is the neck. I often find that people have poor range of motion due to muscle constriction. One of the simplest reasons is the way in which the person breathes.

When we are stuck in our heads and worried or anxious about something, or when we concentrate deeply, we often forget to breathe, hold our breath, or breathe shallowly. When this occurs, the neck muscles become tense and sometimes we even clench our jaws, which can lead to neck tension. (Yes, there are other causes of neck issues as well: accidents, whiplash, etc.) The point I am trying to make is there is one way that you can become more proactive in your own well-being: pay attention to your breath.

One of the most common pieces of advice given in a situation that is emotionally charged or involves conflict is for us to take several deep breaths before speaking. Why? Because giving yourself that extra time can help relax your body and create space in the mind so that clarity can return. Rather then a hasty reaction, a thoughtful response can be articulated. Creating a moment of silence helps to clear the path for your intuition to flow rather than to remain constricted.

Whether you decide to give Tarot readings for others or just use the Tarot for yourself, practicing conscious breath-work will help to ground you and create clarity by bringing you back into the present moment, which strengthens your connection to your intuition.

Your connection with intuition is a connection filled with truth. Your intuition is a gentle voice that is without ego. Just like the breath, intuitive messages come in and out with the regularity and ease of your inhalation and exhalation. Your intuition exists the same way that your breath does. Breathing and intuition just happen. They simply exist within you.

You can develop a deeper connection with your intuition, your breath or both whenever you choose. It just takes willingness and a little practice. In order to connect with your intuition, you must first connect with your breath.

Before beginning this exercise, read through it first and then relax and give it a try.

Part 1.
Connecting to Your Body

Allow yourself to sit up straight and tall. Close your eyes and take a deep breath in through your nose, and then exhale through your nose. Become aware of the expansion that occurs as you inhale. As you take in oxygen, feel your muscles expand and your spine extend up toward the ceiling. Be aware of the muscular contractions that occur with every exhalation. As you expel oxygen, feel your muscles contract or hug closer into your bones. Feel the spaces between the discs in your spine become smaller. As you inhale, you are receiving oxygen, and as you exhale, you are giving carbon monoxide back to the trees and plant life. As you inhale, you receive life, and as you exhale, the plants and trees receive life. Breathing is a constant and beautiful cycle of giving and receiving. Close your eyes and breathe like this for a total of ten deep breaths. Practice being aware of the difference you feel in your muscles when you inhale and exhale. Sink into the experience.

Part 2.
Connecting to Your Intuition

Next, allow yourself to inhale for as long as you can. (Inhale to the point where you cannot take in any more air.) Hold that breath for as long as you can, until it becomes uncomfortable. Now, exhale the breath slowly for as long as possible. When you have reached the end of your exhalation, hold your breath for as long as you can. Do this for three more cycles and then stop.

Take a moment and answer the following questions

1. In which part of the cycle did you experience the most ease? (Inhaling, holding after the inhalation, exhaling, or holding after the exhalation)

2. In which part of the cycle did you experience the least amount of ease? (Inhaling, holding after the inhalation, exhaling, or holding after the exhalation)

3. Where did you spend the most amount of time? (Inhaling, holding after the inhalation, exhaling, or holding after the exhalation)

4. Where did you spend the least amount of time? (Inhaling, holding after the inhalation, exhaling, or holding after the exhalation)

Consider the information offered that follows and compare your answers with the questions listed for each part of the cycle.

The inhalation part of the cycle...

...is related to how you currently receive things in life, your level of creativity and how open you are to new things.

The hold after inhaling...

...symbolizes how comfortable you are with everything you have received, how you express gratitude for what you have received, and how you feel about what you currently have in your life.

The exhalation part of the cycle...

...symbolizes what you are surrendering to in your life and how much you trust just "letting go." (Are you letting go too soon, holding on too long, or withdrawing and not dealing with something?)

The hold after exhaling...

...symbolizes how you deal with the feeling of emptiness in your life, how you experience boredom and how you respond when you have reached a closing chapter in your life and have to start over.

For example: If your answer to question 2 is that you experience the least amount of ease during the inhalation part of the cycle, maybe you are currently uncomfortable with receiving things in your life or your creativity has been low.

This exercise is meant to help you create a deeper insight into yourself.

What new knowledge did you gain?

Part 3.

Creating Balance In Your Body, Mind, & Spirit

Try the exercise from Part 2 while you practice each part of the cycle for the same amount of time. Perhaps you can start by being in each part of the cycle for four seconds: inhaling for four seconds, holding for four seconds, exhaling for four seconds, and holding for four seconds.

Practicing the exercise in this way activates your parasympathetic nervous system and creates an alpha state in your brain. This allows you to feel more creative and open. Remember those instances when you lost all track of time while you were doing something fun or creating/making something? You were producing alpha brain waves. This is a more open and receptive state because your thought process is slower and you exist in the moment, simply aware of the experience at hand. During the day, your brain is usually in a waking or beta state. This is when your thinking mind is very active.

This exercise helps to facilitate a connection between you and your intuition by leading you out of the beta state and guiding you into a more quiet receptive state in your brain. Focusing on the breath is especially effective before giving a reading, when you are feeling stressed, or when you want to be more grounded.

Your path to clarity, peace, and intuition is literally just a few breaths away.

DAY 3

The Autopilot Mode

I remember sitting with my knees hugged to my chest, completely engrossed as my third grade teacher read a passage from *Charlotte's Web*, a children's book by E.B. White. The entire class of twenty children was silent as she read about the adventures of the pig and the spider. Even without pictures, the story had our attention. The words our teacher read created images inside of our heads. We imagined our own version of the barnyard and the animals, and we were completely engrossed in the story, wondering what would happen next.

Stories have an amazing ability to teleport us to another time and place. They are powerful and getting caught up in them can take us to many different worlds. Stories can be real or fictional and can both educate and entertain.

In film, the story has been written and the ending is already determined. Getting lost in a movie's story is wonderful and you can easily be captured by the romance, adventure, or horror onscreen. As you sit and enjoy the buttery smell of popcorn and the salty taste of it in your mouth, as you wash it down with a nice cold carbonated beverage, you allow yourself to go on autopilot as the wonders on the screen unfold.

Similar to the movies, we can get lost or caught up in the themes of our own lives. But our story is a bit different. When we switch into autopilot in our own lives, we forget that we can make different choices. We forget that we can rewrite the theme(s) unfolding in front of us by simply changing our perspective. We forget that we can question our thoughts and recreate our story organically and in the moment.

In our own lives, we are the co-authors and each day we can help choose what words and themes will go on the page. Within our life story, themes or patterns exist. Themes of lost love, adventure, comedy, horror, and tragedy are just a few examples. We can get lost in these stories, go on autopilot, and let an old, outdated storyline take over and repeat itself; or, we can choose to become aware of our outdated thoughts, themes, and patterns and, as a result, rewrite our story.

As you can see, the results created from going on autopilot in a movie theater and going on autopilot with your own life story are very different. Going on autopilot in life is the number one cause for stress. There are several different ways of going on autopilot, but it all boils down to one thing: You forget to factor God into the equation. You forget about Divine intervention and because you believe that life is up to you to figure out, you get tired, frustrated, or ashamed. You choose to go on autopilot and numb out.

The choices that we make when we decide to numb out can keep us repeating the same outdated pattern over and over again. These choices usually include:

* Abuse of alcohol and drugs
* Overindulgence with food or sex
* Escapism through reading, watching television, playing video games, or surfing the Internet for nothing in particular

When we become numb, we forget about Divine intervention, and we lose hope. We start to believe that the hamster wheel we are on is the only path available to us. Then we become stressed and when we are stressed, we continue to surround ourselves with things that help to numb ourselves. In other words, autopilot mode becomes our default setting.

For today, bring awareness to how often you take God out of the equation and go on autopilot. Before you go to bed, take a moment to finish/answer the following:

1. When I felt stress today, I reacted by:

2. After I felt stress, did I numb myself and go on autopilot?

3. How did I attempt to numb myself?

4. How can I let God back in?

Try answering these questions every night for the next two or three weeks. Rather than judging yourself, develop awareness around what causes stress in your life, how often you go on autopilot and the ways in which you numb yourself. This will help you become more present and as a result, offer you support when you decide to do a "rewrite" of your life.

If you have become bored or dissatisfied with your life, you are in the perfect space to make a change. Through this journey, you will learn how to read the Tarot as well as how to rewrite your own personal story. This journey is rich in emotions of all kinds and is only for the courageous. If you have picked up this book, there is a good chance that some part of you is ready to make the change to step more fully into your own authentic life.

DAY 4

The Divine Storyteller

Did you know that some cultures pass down their histories and secrets through oral stories? The tradition of many cultures is to receive history and information from an elder, rather than from a book. The position of the "storyteller" within these cultures and tribes is revered. When a storyteller speaks at a gathering, everybody grows quiet to listen as intently as my third-grade class listened to the story of *Charlotte's Web*.

Your life is full of stories. In fact, you even use the words to describe the events that happen to you as your "life story" and create stories in your mind about the many experiences throughout your lifetime. With the help of intuition, you can utilize the power of your stories to live a bestselling novel. Through an exploration and subsequent understanding of the themes within your personal stories, you can begin to transform your life. When you use your intuition to help others tap into their own stories, you help facilitate the transformation in the lives of others.

Tapping into your intuition allows you to become present not only to your current stories, but to those of another person. As you utilize your intuition, you will hear the voice of an inner narrator or guide. It is a quiet voice—different from the inner judge and critic—the intuitive voice is peaceful, loving, and filled with compassion. Some may call it gut instinct. I like to think of this voice as the voice of God, and I call it the voice of the Divine Storyteller. It is with this voice that you can co-create a life story from a centered space that is full of awareness; you are able to co-create from a space of love and Divine guidance.

Throughout our lives, we often lose track of or stop hearing this Divine voice. This occurs because our inner voice (the ego) becomes louder and drowns out the voice of intuition. The difference between the Divine voice and our ego is that the ego likes to be "right." It is the voice that contains our judgments and criticisms, the voice that tries to convince us that we are not worthy. Do you know how you can tell when the voice of your ego is louder than your Divine voice? When your criticisms, judgments, anger, fear, or anxiety outweigh your feeling of peace, you know the ego is speaking too loudly.

With practice, you can support yourself and others to become a conduit through which the Divine voice may speak. You can choose to channel this voice as an intuitive reader, psychic, medium, or life coach, or you can also choose to channel it to simply live a more peaceful life. When you give a Tarot reading to another person, you have the ability to tap into that person's current stories and themes; you serve as a conduit to help lead the person back to co-creating her/his life as guided by that person's own Divine voice. The Divine voice is the voice of love, and your client's ego is the voice that includes her/his perspectives, opinions, and beliefs. The key is to allow the two voices to work together and co-create a beautiful life story.

While giving a reading, it is important to have compassion when someone's ego is too loud for her/him to hear anything else. The person has gotten lost, stuck or confused in a theme or in part of the story. S/he is repeating a pattern or theme that no longer serves her/his life. As a reader, it is your job to tap into the Divine voice. This action, coupled with communicating the messages you receive, facilitates reconnection to the source of inner peace and knowingness for your client.

Today take part in an activity that allows you to reconnect to your Divine Storyteller. From this point forward, make it a point to incorporate one of these activities as part of your daily practice.

Some Possibilities

- Practice Part 3 (page 25) of the Breath Exercise from Day 2
- Take a walk in nature (in the woods, on the beach)
- Meditate for twenty to thirty minutes
- Visit a church and sit quietly for fifteen minutes
- Watch the sunrise or sunset in silence while breathing slowly
- Take a gentle, yin, or kundalini yoga class

Remember, incorporating these activities/practices help increase your brain's alpha waves, and in this state, more clarity is created. This allows for a direct connection with your intuition and your God source. Living in this state will help you gain awareness of your personal themes so that you can rewrite your life.

Only YOU can answer these questions.

How courageous are you?

How badly do you want to live a better life?

DAY 5

Themes & Filters

As a reader, you support others by tapping into the Divine Storyteller and presenting people with the current themes or patterns that exist in the stories of their lives. Once a Divine connection is reestablished, you can help facilitate possibilities for them to rewrite a bestseller.

Most of the time, people choose to have readings because they are lost in part of their story, or they have a few stories that need clarification. The conversations they have with themselves or others are out of sync with their dreams. In other words, their egos have run a-muck. They begin to suspect that something is off and a part of them starts to seek clarity and reconnection. When people are lost in their story, they need to be reminded to go within and reconnect to their "God source." Reconnecting reminds them that they are not alone, that something higher and greater supports them.

When people have a few stories running, they may explore choices with the hope of narrowing down a course of action. Clients will come to you to explore the possibilities present in their lives.

The word "reading" is appropriate because, with the help of the Divine Storyteller, we, as readers, serve to orate or read people's past and current stories aloud to them. We also offer insight into their future stories. When one receives a reading, s/he is reminded that a magnificent God offers support; all one has to do is tap in and ask for help.

Oftentimes, clients request readings when they notice the way in which they have been doing something no longer serves them. This happens when they realize that the way they view and react to a situation is creating stagnation or chaos rather than simplicity. Their environment and experiences have helped to form their beliefs, which are filters or lenses through which they view their stories. As these clients begin to question their beliefs, they realize that their filters need to be cleaned. The egoless voice of the Divine Storyteller helps to provide the clarity for which they have been seeking.

The filters through which we view our lives have helped to create patterns, which lead to a sense of order, which in turn can establish comfort. As humans, we create patterns in an effort to make logical sense of our lives. It is when we get stuck in our patterns that we get stuck in our stories.

When someone seeks a reading, on some level that person realizes that s/he has become stuck. The Divine Storyteller can go beyond the roadblocks of that person's inner storyteller to help create a sacred revision of the story.

Patterns develop themes/situations, and themes create stories. The themes within our situations are the repetitive inner messages we develop that prevent us or encourage us throughout our lives. These themes prevent us from moving forward unless we view them as opportunities from which we can learn and grow. As we begin to view life as a series of short stories, we walk on the path that will allow us to tap into our intuitive selves. By looking closely at our beliefs and actions, we discover our themes.

Our childhood years are the formative years for our beliefs, patterns, and themes. To help illustrate, I will share an example from my childhood. When I grew up, I lived with my family in a trailer. My parents divorced when I was ten and, until I left for college, I lived with my mother and brother, and the three of us were supported by the Welfare system. Both of my parents constantly worried about money. I grew up surrounded by the fears of scarcity, poverty, and lack. As a result, one of my themes became: "I will never have enough or be enough."

As I explore this theme and choose to connect with the Divine Storyteller, I have a chance to test my boundaries and create perspective shifts. This personal work has inspired me to offer this support to others. When I give a reading for another and help reconnect that person to the Divine Storyteller, I create the opportunity for that person to have a similar experience, and I love that!

Exploring Your Themes Exercise

To explore your own themes or recurring messages, think back to when you were growing up and living under someone else's roof. My examples are shown in italics.

1. Write down a message that your parents (or the adults around you) consistently repeated about loving relationships, work or money.

My parent's message: Rich people think that they are better than us.

2. What have you learned from the views of society, your peers, and the media on this particular subject?

Money is power.

3. What beliefs emerged from the messages that were shared?

Too much money will make me think I am better than anyone else. Money = Power; therefore, money and power are bad.

4. How do these beliefs affect your current life story?

If money and power are bad, I shouldn't have too much of either. I should just have enough to get by.

5. How do these themes support your current life story:

    Physically?

I need to work harder and for less than I am worth because that is my lot in life. As a result, I am always tired and have little time for fun.

Emotionally?

I feel anxious whenever I have too much or too little money.

Mentally?

My sense of power is equated to the amount of money that I have. So, others who have more then me are better then me.

Spiritually?

I blame God and myself for making me poor.

6. How do these messages lead to limitations in your life?

I have no boundaries on the amount of hours that I work because I determine my own worth based on the amount of work I do. If I am not working, then I am worthless.

7. Are the messages that were shared with you true?

Are all wealthy people better than me? No, that is a generalization.

8. What is the new message you would like to share with yourself?

Money is neither good nor bad. I get to decide how to use it. My worth is determined by how I am, not what I have.

[See the Appendix for another listing of these questions.] Take a few moments and write down whatever comes to mind. Remember that you are developing a deeper relationship with yourself; once you begin to understand and articulate your underlying beliefs, you can begin to help rewrite your stories with the help of your God source.

After you answer these questions, you will begin to see how the messages you learned have led to beliefs, which, along with how you have chosen to live, have created themes. Pay attention to the areas in your own life where you experience limitations or constriction.

What themes keep replaying?

DAY 6

Comfort In Our Discomfort

Intuitive readers are those who willingly tap into another person's story. They become orators, allowing the Divine Storyteller to speak through them. The person receiving the reading then decides how the rewrite will happen, as well as how to more fully participate in her/his own bestseller. The most important component to the creation of a bestseller is choice. Each of us has the choice to explore boundaries and question our current themes. The choice is not always an easy one, as one's ego can step in because it wants to defend the person's old themes and patterns.

As humans, we find comfort in our patterns and themes, creating routines that are like pathways. Each time the pathways are traveled, the indentations they create grow deeper. We, in turn, travel these deeply formed pathways out of habit. We begin to follow these ruts automatically because we receive comfort in the repetition and, over time, we defend the ruts because to follow the well-worn path is easier than creating a new pathway. Receiving a reading sheds light on current ruts or recurring themes.

Our comfort with these ruts causes us to become attached to our themes, which the ego will protect with a vengeance. When we try to break a habit, we fight with the part of ourselves that has become attached to the habit. When we try to "break" a habit, our ego reacts because it fears "breaking" that to which it has become attached. Rather than believing that you are breaking a pattern, tell yourself that you are shifting into another pattern, one that better serves your current life story.

You can view such a transition the following way: when driving a car with a manual transmission, you purposely shift the gears. You cannot change from first to fourth gear without using the clutch before shifting. Similarly, changing one's theme involves finding the clutch that supports a smooth transition from one story line to another. That clutch is faith in our God source to help us find a better pathway on the journey to serve the highest good.

I know that I sometimes get lost in my own themes and get lazy. I become comfortable in the ruts I have created. The decision to change my theme would require doing something different, something unknown. The beauty of this, however, is that once I have made a commitment to connect to my faith and my God source, change becomes easier. When I alter my actions and surrender my old themes to my God source, a new pattern/theme forms. This new theme is more loving; it creates more self-esteem and a stronger feeling of self-worth. Once I get too attached to this theme, I may be guided to change it in the future as well. It helps me to remember that I am "a work in progress."

As you tap into your intuition or give a reading, you create an opportunity to change outdated themes. Sometimes, the only way the Divine Storyteller can get our attention is by creating an event that is so profound we are forced to see it. This happens when we have become very stuck in our themes and refuse to let go of them. Examples of this could include a crisis with our health, our emotions, or our finances. Why does it take a crisis to create change? Sometimes, the best motivator to change a theme is fear of physical death or reaching the absolute bottom of one's perceived abilities.

When we learn to connect to the Divine Storyteller on a regular basis and remain open to changing an outdated theme, we can avoid these extremes. Sometimes, a crisis will occur regardless because the event was meant as a lesson for all involved. The ability to stay connected to the Divine Storyteller during a crisis can help us remain present, grounded, and clear as we make new choices to effectively support a revision of the story.

Some of the best motivators to change a theme are fear, frustration, and anger. Rather than withdrawing from unpleasant emotions, we can use them to move forward. Unpleasant emotions make us uncomfortable, and it is during these times of discomfort that we are out of integrity. What we need to do is take an honest look at our discomfort, allow ourselves to experience it, and allow the feelings to flow through us.

Perhaps we are uncomfortable because it is time to let go of our current theme. When we look deeper, we may find that our discomfort is a clue that strives to tell us it is time to change. Exploring the discomfort is important. Are we holding onto a theme that supports a story of love and possibility, or does the theme continue to cause constriction? When you feel discomfort in regards to change, ask yourself what you protect by sticking with your current theme. Dig deeper to find out if the protection is necessary for the survival of your spirit or the survival of your ego.

Whenever I give a reading, I take time to feel gratitude for what is about to unfold and be shown to me. The opportunity to be a channel for the story to flow through, and to be trusted as a conduit for Divine support, is pretty amazing. The ability to offer the opportunity of self-examination to another is a gift. Even as I write this and think about this opportunity, I am humbled.

Today or tomorrow, when you find yourself following a familiar pattern, do something to change it and take notice of what comes up for you. For example: take a different route when driving to work, pick a different item on the menu at your favorite restaurant, or take a bath instead of a shower. When you make a different choice, notice any resistance that you feel and just breathe through it. Building awareness and using your breath to practice resilience will help you face resistance rather than withdrawing from it and creating deep ruts.

DAY 7
Using Your Words

I had just turned thirty when a friend invited me to dinner. She wanted to introduce me to her friend, a man who had left the corporate world to become a monk. He was an inspiration to her, and she wanted me to experience some time in his presence. We met at a restaurant close to the monastery where he lived.

Upon meeting this man, I immediately felt peaceful and relaxed. As we waited for our dinner to arrive, he asked me what I wanted to do with my life. I shared my dream to move to California and become a massage therapist. I thought that I could use my intuition in the massage field and that by becoming a Holistic Health Practitioner and massage therapist, I would get more education and pursue a job that was more credible than simply giving readings.

By that time, I had put readings on the back burner and focused instead on receiving respect from the amount of degrees and certificates that I could earn. I thought that people would take me more seriously if I had framed certificates on my wall and that, with more degrees, I could help more people. After I finished telling this man my idea, this peaceful being asked me if he could perform energy work on me. I quickly agreed and he stood behind my chair, placing one hand behind my head and one over my forehead. It felt like I was a baby being rocking gently to sleep. My mind became clear after a few moments he removed his hands, smiled gently at me and said, "You can heal with your words."

As I left dinner that night, I was still determined to follow what I had deemed the path to credibility, but those words stayed with me. It wasn't until years later I began to understand what that sentence meant. In that moment, the Divine had communicated through him to let me know that the words I chose to use through my readings were also my power. While I had thought I could offer healing in one way, he pointed out that healing could also happen through the words that I used when I gave readings. As I look back now, I can see that this one sentence turned my life into a quest to understand the power behind language and words.

Our words form the stories in which we live. We use words not only in our internal dialogue, but also when we speak aloud. Our words are powerful and can be used to rewrite our stories. When we give a reading and connect to the Divine Storyteller, the words that come through us can be used to create expansion and facilitate healing for others.

When we speak to others and ourselves, the words we choose define who we are and how we live. Unfortunately, sometimes we use words that harm rather than heal. Healing begins with love, and the use of a loving vocabulary is supportive; it opens up a space for healing to begin. This is especially important when one has become less than kind with one's internal dialogue.

When you give a reading, you allow yourself to be a conduit through which the loving words of the Divine Storyteller can travel. The intention behind the teachings in this book is about being a conduit and giving that gift of love to the person receiving the reading.

When a person comes to you for a reading, that person seeks to reconnect with something larger than the self, to be reminded to love more fully, to go deeper within, and to gain confirmation that her/his current path is a good one. Receiving a reading reconnects someone to the Divine Storyteller, as a reading reminds the receiver of possibility and hope. Hope then helps the recipient reconnect to her/his faith, and when faith in the Divine Storyteller is renewed, the recipient's filters can change. Through this reconnection to the idea that one is a part of something greater, one can examine her/his filters more clearly and eventually change one's actions. This ultimately leads to a shift on the themes or situations in one's life.

Take a moment and write out your intentions for reading the Tarot for yourself and others. Begin by finishing this statement:

I intend to tap into my intuition and give readings

to myself and others in order to:

DAY 8
Faith & Hope

Faith is the key ingredient for tapping into your intuition, reading Tarot cards and rewriting the new bestseller of your life. Faith is the glue that unites you with joy and bliss; it is about believing that your God source walks beside you and helps you co-create your personal revision. When faith is lost, you become contracted, which allows your ego to take over, leading to a fuzzy connection to the Divine Storyteller.

In a sense, a domino effect begins to occur: your faith affects your beliefs, which affect the filters through which you view the story of your life. Your filters, in turn, influence your actions, while those actions create patterns or themes. When you reconnect with the Divine Storyteller, your hope is restored and faith begins to breathe again. The reason I love to give readings is because I am able to reconnect people with their faith, hope, and the Divine Storyteller (their God source).

When you connect to the Divine Storyteller, you enter a space of "no filters," a space of ultimate faith that is separate from your own beliefs. A connection with the Divine Storyteller reminds you that dreams are possible. When you give a reading, your opinions and filters are placed on hold.

At this point, what flows though you is the voice of the Divine Storyteller, who observes the unfolding story and reoccurring themes, reminding you or your client that one can do a rewrite and live a more fulfilling, faith-filled life.

Get to know difference between the Divine Storyteller and your ego. When you do this, you will transform your life and the lives of others.

Voice of Ego	Voice of Divine Storyteller
I'm too old.	Trust Divine Timing
I'm not good enough.	You are worth it.
I have to do it, or I'll feel guilty.	Is your choice for the highest good of all involved?
What if I fail?	There are no mistakes, only lessons.
I'm ugly, fat, dumb, etc.	You are perfect.
I'm alone.	I'm here. You are loved.
Why did this happen to me?	What lesson did you learn from what happened?
What am I going to do?	Surrender the situation to me and ask for Divine Guidance.

Take some time today and tomorrow to observe your thoughts. See if you can recognize the difference between the voice of your ego and that of the Divine Storyteller.

Is there a common emotion or

theme that you begin to notice?

What will help you reconnect to your faith and hope?

HINT: *What daily spiritual practice(s) have you committed to?*

DAY 9

What is Intuition, Anyway?

W hat is intuition? It is an inner knowingness, a quiet voice that speaks to you when you clear away the clutter in your mind. Intuition grows stronger as you connect to your faith. Some people describe it as a gut feeling or a hunch. The simple fact is that everyone has intuition; we were all born with it. How you decide to develop it is your choice.

This book is about intuition, and it's direct connection to God, a connection to that which is formless and greater than you. It is a voice filled with truth, which silences the ego and reminds the listener of possibility and expansion. When people choose to get a reading, they are usually stuck, contracted, or seeking clarity. They are asking to be reminded of other possibilities that may exist for them.

When you are working with others as a reader, it is essential to remove your opinions, the "me" (ego), from the equation. When you don't remove the "me," you speak through your filters and merely give your point of view. When the "me" is removed and the Divine Storyteller is tapped, the messages that filter through create expansion and possibility. The voice that speaks through you is one of love and compassion.

This is why connection to and the ability to serve as a conduit for the Divine Storyteller (God source) is essential. You are better able to communicate the current contractions or blockages in your clients' lives. The Divine Storyteller will then remind clients how they can change their theme and live the story of their dreams. The Divine Storyteller offers expansion to that which has become contracted.

The act of connection with the Divine Storyteller is a great practice. Whether you choose to do it for your own day-to-day life or to help support others, the clarity that emerges is beneficial for all involved. The following practice will help you connect to the Divine Storyteller and will be helpful to you not only as a reader, but also in your everyday life.

Holding Space

Today or tomorrow, when someone chooses to confide in you, give him or her your complete attention. Listen to what that person says, and each time you want to give an opinion, say something like "I know," or if you find that you want to share a similar story, stop yourself. Instead, continue to listen until the person is finished speaking or asks for a response.

Each time you want to interrupt or add your comments, take a few breaths and wait for the person to pause. When s/he does, ask yourself the following questions before offering your comments:

1. Will my comments cause expansion or contraction for this person?

2. Am I supporting this person in writing a more loving story?

3. What questions can I ask or what comments can I offer to support this person in writing a more loving story?

Taking the "Me" Out of the Equation

When listening and offering support to another person, how do you know that the answers do not come from your ego? How will you know when you are channeling the Divine Storyteller? In my experience, when I give a reading, it is very clear to me when the Divine Storyteller steps in because the speed at which I speak changes. In my everyday life, my speaking pattern is more slow or methodical; I listen more than I speak. However, when I give a reading, my speaking pattern is quicker and more matter-of-fact. When I give a reading, a great deal of information tends to come through at once, which causes me to speak more quickly. It is as if I speak faster than the "me" inside can form thoughts.

Your process may be the same, or it may be completely different. To begin the process of self-discovery, bring attention to the way that the connection to the Divine works for you. Notice the difference between the voice of your own inner narrator and the voice of the Divine Storyteller, God.

DAY 10

Right or Left Brained?

Your ego took its first breath when you were born as it immediately began digesting and processing the stimuli around you. Then, your nervous system processed and recorded the places, people, conversations, and emotions you experienced, and these memories were filed away as stories that you would relive in your head throughout your life. In fact, your ego is a voice that you will continue to hear until you take your last breath. It processes the many stimuli that you experience as it critiques each moment as "good" or "bad." Your beliefs are formed, and they have created and continue to create filters or "a point of view." Your life story is interpreted through these filters and as a result, reoccurring themes or patterns present themselves in your life.

The ego is most active when you are trapped in thoughts of the past or anxieties about the future. Present moment awareness (when you are practicing breath-work, meditating, or working on a creative project) is the one thing that helps to silence your ego's voice and creates room so that you can hear the voice of the Divine. When you can get away from the judgments of whether a situation is "good" or "bad" and, instead, just be in a given situation, you are able to change your story. The story can change when you access your intuition and connect with your God source.

We are all born with a direct connection to God, but our ego steps in and diverts us away from the Divine voice. Your job as a reader is to become the conduit of the Divine voice so that you can question the beliefs and themes of the ego. Whether it is your ego or your client's, these beliefs and themes can be brought to the light and examined.

Your brain is divided into two halves, which create two perspectives for you to access. The left side of your brain is responsible for your logical/rational perspective, and the right side pertains to your intuitive/creative perspective. Structure, order, logic, and timing are important to the left side of the brain, whereas art, intuition, and creativity are important to your right. Sometimes, you view life more from one perspective than the other.

Exclusive existence in the left side perspective creates a direct connection to one's ego, while exclusive existence in the right side perspective creates a direct connection to your God source. As we were born with a body, we need to create balance between the two hemispheres of the brain as we strive to live a God-centered, intuitive life in our bodies.

Are you more LEFT-brained or RIGHT-brained? To see which hemisphere you favor, read the following statements and circle the ones that apply to you.

LEFT Brain statements:

- I believe in right and wrong.
- I like following written directions.
- Sticking to a schedule is important.
- I wear a wristwatch and often consult it to make sure I am on time.
- I am always on time.
- I set goals and follow through to achieve goals.
- I consider the pros and cons of a situation.
- I like to get all of the facts before I make a decision.

RIGHT Brain statements:

- I love to write poetry or paint.
- I enjoy metaphors.
- Schedules make me feel trapped.
- I trust my gut instincts.
- I am often late.
- I use my hands a lot when I talk.
- I lose track of time easily.
- I enjoy inventing new recipes.

The approach to intuition that is explored in this book marries the viewpoints of both sides of your brain. As you explore intuition, you will be led to mix the left side approach (understanding your themes and filters; setting goals and action plans for yourself or your clients) with the right side approach (breathing; quieting your mind; and getting to know what you personally associate with each card).

As there are many resources available for the meanings and stories behind the cards, this book focuses on the right-side approach. Reconnecting with your God source while living your life and facilitating a healing space for others is more important than facilitating that space from your ego. Besides, let's face it: aren't you a little intimidated by the thought of just memorizing seventy-eight cards before you give a reading? Utilizing both your logical and creative sides develop your intuition from a grounded place. This approach can be used to live life, tap into your intuition and read the Tarot. By doing this, your experiences will be richer and more complete.

Day 11

No Need to Compare

When I first began giving readings, I constantly questioned my abilities and continually compared the way I gave readings to the way of others. (Remember my theme of "never being enough?") I wondered why I did not see auras or spirits like my teacher and why I received messages differently than my other intuitive friends. Because my way was unusual compared to others, I thought that I was not as good. Later, I came to realize that these thoughts were as ridiculous as other beliefs: that being a certain height makes you smarter, or the ability to speak a certain language makes you superior to someone who speaks a different one. I understood that the way in which I received and shared messages was as valid as the way others received and shared messages. The way in which each of us receives intuitive messages is as unique as we are.

See Hear

Feel Know

When tapping into your intuition, the way you receive information may vary from the way others around you receive it. By understanding how your intuition works and the language in which the Divine Storyteller speaks, you can perfect your intuition and decide if you want to explore other methods. Tapping into your intuition and connecting with the Divine Storyteller enables you to see, hear, feel, or know information on a level that is deeper than that which is experienced by the casual observer. For the purpose of this book, we will explore the four deeper ways of receiving messages that consist of seeing, hearing, feeling, and just knowing.

Seeing

Do you see images or pictures in your head or in front of you? Do you see colors around someone? Do you dream of or get flashes of past or future events? When you receive messages in a visual way, this is called clairvoyance.

Hearing

Do you hear words or phrases? Do you hear a name? Do you hear a sound (for example, a fire engine) when you think about a personal relationship? When your messages come through in an auditory way, this is called clairaudience.

Feeling

Do you feel what others are feeling? Do you feel things in your body when you think of a particular person or when you are asked health-related questions? Do you get a feeling in the pit of your stomach? When your messages come through in an experiential or "feeling" way, this is called clairsentience.

Knowing

Do you just know the answer? When another person asks you a question, does an answer come through quickly, in a matter-of-fact way, without any thought on your part? Do you think of an issue and just "know" the answer? Perhaps you receive an entire sentence or phrase regarding something about which you previously had no known knowledge. When your messages come through this way, it is called claircognizance.

All methods that connect you to the Divine Storyteller are valid, as the connection with the Divine is one filled with truth. It is a gentle language that is without ego.

While there are other ways to receive your information, clairvoyance, clairaudience, clairsentience, and claircognizance are the most common ones. They are all wonderful ways of receiving messages and one is no better than the other. The language in which the Divine Storyteller communicates to you is your native tongue. Just like learning a new language, any of these methods can be learned, utilized, and strengthened. It is your choice to explore and enjoy whichever ones you would like.

Everyone has the ability to tap into his or her intuition. We were all born with intuition as part of the package. Similar to muscles, intuition can be toned and strengthened. It is up to you whether you choose to utilize it or not. How does the Divine Storyteller communicate through you?

Practices for Strengthening

the Four Abilities

Find a space where you will not be interrupted and take a comfortable seat. Then, practice Part 3 (page 25) from Day 2 for five minutes before starting each exercise.

Strengthening Clairvoyance

Sit down with a piece of paper and pen. Pick any room in your house and write the name of the room at the top of the page. Next, close your eyes for one full minute and imagine the room. When you are done, open your eyes and, without looking around, write down the details of the room. Describe it in as many minute details as possible. Include the number of walls, their texture and color, the placement of furniture, the objects in the room, etc. Use adjectives generously and when you describe an object or piece of furniture, describe how and where it is placed.

> **Example**: There is a maple bookshelf with five shelves on the west wall of the living room. The first shelf contains three books (name of books here) and two red four-inch pillar candles that are burning. The candles are to the right of the books and in the center of the shelf. There is only one other object on the shelf and it is to the right of the candles; it is a deck of Tarot cards in a wooden, flowered box.

Close your eyes as often as you would like and bring the images back onto the screen in your mind. Have fun with this practice and see how many details you can remember. This is the practice of seeing objects in your mind.

Strengthening Clairaudience

Find a place where you can sit down comfortably. As you close your eyes, begin to notice the different sounds that you hear. As you hear two or three, open your eyes and write down the sounds you have identified. Be aware of the many sounds that surround you. Continue with this exercise until you have heard and recorded ten to fifteen different sounds.

Have fun with this and over time, increase the number of different sounds that you hear. This is the practice of hearing on a deeper level.

Strengthening Clairsentience

This can be done before preparing a meal at home or before ordering a meal at a restaurant. Close your eyes and imagine what you are thinking of eating. Ask your body what it will feel like to eat this particular meal. Pay attention to the signals. Are you getting a satisfied feeling? An uncomfortable or heavy feeling? After you have eaten, compare the way you actually feel to the way you felt when you imagined the food.

In the future, you may choose to practice imagining a meal until you feel a comfortable sensation in your stomach and, eventually, that sensation will match how you actually feel afterwards. This tool is useful for the digestive process. Over time, you may even find that you make healthier eating choices. This is the practice of feeling at a deeper level.

Strengthening Claircognizance

Sit down with a piece of paper and pen. Think of a situation in your life around which you would like to gain clarity, and write a short note with the question to your God source (see example below):

Dear Divine Storyteller,

What is the best course of action to take regarding my career? I give you permission to communicate through my pen onto this paper. Thank you for your guidance.

Put the pen down, and take three to five minutes to practice the Conscious Breathing Exercise. Now, pick up your pen and allow your God source to write a note, through your hand, back to you. Begin by addressing the response to yourself and just let the rest flow through you.

Have fun with this and over time, you may notice that you merely have to think the question, and then after you practice Part 3 (page 25) from Day 2, the answer comes through without writing it down. This is the practice of knowing at a deeper level.

Connecting with our breath is an excellent way to connect with our God source because through this connection, we are free from the daily chatter and thoughts that cloud our minds. When we give a reading with the purpose of facilitating reconnection for another, we are also free from our story. To be a great reader, it is essential to have a practice in place that helps you free yourself from the chatter of the mind.

Freedom from your mind chatter serves two purposes. The first is to help you connect with the Divine Storyteller regularly and live a life that is grounded with more awareness. The second is to help you become a clear channel to facilitate the healing of another. Breath-work and meditation assist to facilitate a quick connection to the Divine Storyteller. Practicing Part 3 (page 25) from Day 2 for five minutes is an excellent, quick way to create clarity and become a conduit so that the Divine Storyteller can flow through you.

Meditation is another great practice to help clear mind chatter. Becoming a clear conduit is the first step in tapping into your intuition; one must choose a supportive practice in order to facilitate this process.

Intuition, or that voice of the Divine Storyteller, is a quiet voice that is full of clarity. This voice is clear from judgments, criticisms, advice, or negativity. The ability to access it involves a compassionate and unconditional way of seeing, hearing, feeling, and knowing.

When you begin to have thoughts that agree, disagree, or question the messages, if you start thinking "this is right" or "this is wrong," your ego has entered the picture. On the contrary, when the messages flow through you as effortlessly as breath, your ego has stepped aside. You are merely the conduit—the vessel through which the story flows. The way in which you receive those messages is unique to you.

Your connection to the Divine Storyteller will come more easily when you understand how your intuition works, develop practices that create clarity in your mind, and strengthen your "clairs." These practices will also deepen your confidence in your ability to help others. As this occurs, you will enjoy rewriting your own bestseller, as well as facilitating the space for others to rewrite theirs.

DAY 12
Signs & Symbols
(Part One)

If you haven't already guessed, reading the Tarot starts with connecting to and channeling your God source. You are ready to continue now that you have a better understanding of how the Divine Storyteller speaks to you. The first and most crucial step on this journey is for you to understand that the information is coming *through* you and not *from* you. Even though your voice may be telling the story, you and your ego are stepping out of the way; you are merely a conduit for something greater. When you embrace this belief, the process becomes simple and effortless.

As you allow your God source to flow through you, the story becomes about the person in front of you and not about whether you are right or wrong about the stories that your voice is sharing. Rather than worry about being right or wrong, relax and ride the flow. The stories/messages will come through you when you allow the process to occur. Trust in the process is more important to the reading than memorization of the cards. If you remember the connection with your God source, the trust in the Divine will always trump the ego's need to be right.

Once you are open and you allow yourself to ride the wave, the story will flow through you. On Day 11, you began to explore and understand how one receives messages from the Divine Storyteller. Once you have embraced the understanding and acquaint yourself with your deck, you can begin to share the transmission with your clients. By channeling the Divine Storyteller, you will share your clients' current stories and themes with them. By doing this, you become the conduit for your clients' current stories or dreams to unfold out loud and in front of them.

Have you heard of dream interpretation? Think of life stories as a series of dreams that you experience during your waking state. You have the power to interpret those as easily as the dreams you have while asleep. All you have to do is tap into your intuition and the Divine Storyteller. This places you on the path to expanding your self-awareness and intuition. Better self-awareness and connection to your God source is a recipe for success as a reader.

Within our life stories, we develop patterns or themes. When we give a reading, we pave the way to become a clear conduit for the Divine Storyteller, and we tap into the symbols and themes that present themselves in the our own lives and the lives of our clients in the waking state. The Divine Storyteller is the dream interpreter, and you are the conduit.

Part of the ability to be the voice for this dream interpretation resides in understanding the symbols that are presented in the dream or story. When you learn the art of giving a reading or becoming a conduit for the Divine Storyteller, it is important to establish your own personal dream

interpretation guide. Part Two of this book will acquaint you with your deck and teach you how to use it as your main tool for dream interpretation.

As we wrap up Part One of this book, let's start with a simple understanding of symbols and associations. Here is an example: let's say that you associate a butterfly as a symbol of joy, and you can ask your God source/the Divine Storyteller to show you a butterfly during a reading to indicate joy. So, when someone asks you a question about her/his love life and your eyes are drawn to a butterfly on one of your Tarot cards, you can interpret the answer to the question as a union that is full of joy.

Signs & Symbols Exercise

The next time you are out on a walk, think of a question about which you would like some clarity. Then, ask the Divine Storyteller to send you a sign or symbol to help clarify your issue. Start practicing the breath-work from Day 2 (page 25) as you walk. Once you have practiced for three to five minutes, look around. The breath-work helps facilitate a deeper-level awareness within you. From this state, view the world around you. Does a word or phrase on a billboard or bumper sticker command your attention? Do you hear the sound of laughter or maybe a siren? Does someone step up out of the blue and say something to you? Do you see an animal or insect? Did you hear part of a song? Are you led to go somewhere different on your walk? Do you feel the wind pick up? Do you feel a chill? Does it start to rain? What do you see, hear, feel or know in this present state of awareness?

During this exercise, resist the urge to search for signs and symbols; instead, simply receive them.

The Signs & Symbols exercise is a great practice as you first begin to explore how the right side of your brain approaches a reading. Assigning your own meanings and creating your own dream interpretation guide soothes the left (organized and orderly) side of your brain. Utilizing both the right and left brains when giving a reading combines the inner trust that a natural flow exists with your knowledge of the meanings behind numbers, colors, and symbols. Trust and knowledge, combined with a good personal dream interpretation guide, guarantees a great reading.

DAY 13

Signs & Symbols
(Part Two)

During my training as a massage therapist, I was given a valuable piece of advice that I have applied to several areas in my life thereafter. The instructor at my school spent many hours teaching us a variety of modalities and techniques. On the last day of class, before our practical exam, he said, "Now forget everything you know or think you know, and just do it."

That being said, there are many excellent references that one can access to learn the history and meaning behind the colors, number, and symbols of the Tarot. Learning the history behind these colors, numbers, and symbols and memorizing the meaning of the cards satisfies the left-brain, and it also activates that need to do things correctly. So, instead of memorizing anything, we will approach learning the Tarot from the right side to see what your intuition is currently telling you. Take a moment to complete the following exercise, which begins to develop a connection between you, your intuition, and your deck.

Before starting this exercise, practice your conscious breathing exercise from Day 2 (page 25) for three to five minutes.

As you read each of the following words, write down three words that you associate with each listed word; just let the answers flow through you. Regardless of what words come through, just write. This is the practice of being a conduit and connecting to the flow of Divine information.

Color	Association
Red	
Orange	
Yellow	

Green	
Blue	
Purple	
White	
Brown	
Black	
Grey	
Gold	
Silver	

Stop, and once again practice your conscious breath-work for three to five minutes. As you read each of the following words, write down three words that you associate with each listed word; just let the answers flow through you.

Number	Association
Zero (0)	
One (1)	
Two (2)	
Three (3)	
Four (4)	
Five (5)	
Six (6)	

Seven (7)	
Eight (8)	
Nine (9)	
Ten (10)	

Stop, and once again practice your conscious breath-work for three to five minutes. As you read each of the following words, write down three words that you associate with each listed word; just let the answers flow through you.

Word	Association
Water	
Fire	
Earth	

Air	
King	
Queen	
Knight	
Page	

The beauty of the Tarot is that each card in the deck holds a story. It is a story that will flow through you as you connect and allow yourself to be a conduit. Each card has a unique set of colors, symbols, numbers, people, or animals. The combined use of colors and symbols give the card a certain "feel." Each card has its own action/story that takes place within its borders.

Gaining an understanding of your own associations with colors, numbers, and symbols is the first step in connecting with your deck. Much like riding a bike, once that rapport is developed, it never disappears.

DAY 14

Recapitulation

Before we move on to connecting with our deck, let's take a day just to review what we have learned up to this point. Make notes.

1. Good rest, a daily spiritual practice, regular exercise, and good nutrition are essential for your vitality. The more energized you are, the more receptive you will be to that quiet voice of intuition. What daily practices are you finding helpful on your journey so far?

2. Your path to clarity, peace, and intuition is literally a few breaths away. Are you finding the breath-work from Day Two helpful? If you have your own form that you prefer to practice, feel free to utilize it. There are entire courses of study dedicated to the breath. Enjoy the exploration.

3. Develop awareness rather than judgments of your own patterns.

4. When any thought related to criticism, judgment, anger, fear, or anxiety outweighs your feelings of peace and love, you are in your ego.

5. Exploring your themes while connecting with your God source will give you a chance to test your boundaries and create perspective shifts.

6. If you are experiencing constriction in an area of your life, there are probably outdated themes and patterns in repetition right now.

7. When you feel discomfort regarding change, dig deeper to find out if you are protecting your spirit or if you are protecting your ego.

8. When speaking to someone ask yourself: "Am I using my words to harm or heal?"

9. How do you stay connected to your faith and hope?

10. Everyone has intuition; you are merely a conduit through which the information flows. The way that you receive the messages is unique to you.

11. Forget everything you know or think you know; connect to your God source and just let the messages flow through you.

Now that the groundwork has been laid, you are ready to work with the seventy-eight Tarot cards within your deck. During the next part of this book, you will focus on your cards and the story contained within each one. You will become familiar with the cards, learn how to read them, and allow the messages of the Divine Storyteller to flow through you without rote memorization of particular card meanings.

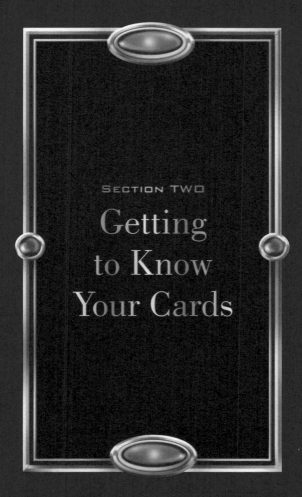

SECTION TWO

Getting
to Know
Your Cards

DAY 15

Major vs. Minor

I t's time to start connecting with your deck. Beginning today, you will want to keep your deck handy for each day's lesson. We will dig in and create your dream interpretation guide for the waking dream we all live. As we begin, two well-known sayings come to mind:

"Let go, and let God."

and

"Just do it."

These quotes apply to the two main segments in the Tarot deck: the Major and the Minor Arcana. There are seventy-eight cards within the Tarot deck; twenty-two cards are Major Arcana cards, and fifty-six are Minor Arcana cards. The word "arcana" is often defined as "a secret or a mystery." The specific way in which the cards fall during a reading determines which motto one should embrace.

The "Just do it" motto applies when a majority of Minor Arcana appear in a reading. These cards let the querent (or person asking the question) know that the situation or story is in her/his hands. It is up to that person to take action. Sometimes during a reading, an action plan unfolds, the querent leaves with the intention of devising an action plan or following through on a plan that is already in the works.

When a majority of Major Arcana cards appear in a reading, it is time to for the querent to "Let go and let God." In this case, the cards indicate that the wheels of fate are at work and that it is time to for one to sit back and watch it unfold. The situation is in God's hands. This is not a time of doing, but rather a time of surrendering the situation to your God source as you observe and receive with a sense of patience.

Give this theory a try for yourself. Pick up your deck and think of a present situation in your life around which you would like clarity. Focus your thoughts on this situation as you shuffle the cards. When it feels right, stop shuffling, choose three cards from the deck, turn them over and look at them. Now, take a moment and answer the following questions.

THE SUN

TWO OF WANDS

THE HIGH PRIESTESS

NINE OF PENTACLES

The three cards I pulled were:

1.

2.

3.

The majority of cards were from the (Major or Minor) _____ Arcana.

This means that it is up to me to:

Now, notice what colors, numbers, or symbols command your attention.

Three things that I noticed on each of the cards were:

Card #1:

Card #2:

Card #3:

Turn back to Day 14 and look at the meanings you wrote down regarding symbols and colors. Did you mention any of these meanings when you chose three things from each card above? Besides the knowledge that you either need to take action or surrender, what other messages are shown by the story portrayed on the card? Take a moment and just write the answers as they come through you.

The messages being shown to me in this moment are:

The Minor Arcana

"God, grant me the serenity to accept the things I cannot change, courage to change the things I can, and wisdom to know the difference."

—Reinhold Niebuhr

"The Serenity Prayer" refers to the importance of finding the balance between surrender and action, being and doing, and the Major and Minor Arcanas. The first part of the prayer refers to the Major Arcana and the importance of surrendering to Divine Will. The second part, "courage to change the things I can," refers to the Minor Arcana and the idea that one must devise an action plan to move forward.

The Minor Arcana cards in a Tarot deck are similar to modern-day playing cards, as both decks have four suits. The Minor Arcana's four suits are: cups, rods, swords, and pentacles, whereas modern-day playing cards use the four suits of hearts, clubs, spades, and diamonds. In the Tarot deck, the cups correspond to the suit of hearts; the rods/wands/staffs to clubs; the swords to spades; and the pentacles/coins to diamonds.

Modern-day playing cards have numbered cards (one through ten) and a Jack, Queen, and King in each suit. The Minor Arcana have numbered cards (one through ten) and four court cards. The court cards include a Page, Knight, Queen, and King. This is the only difference in the two decks, which, as you will see later, is important.

Each suit in the Minor Arcana also symbolizes an element. Today we will begin to explore the suits and their symbols. For now, just be aware that when the Minor Arcana show up in a reading and outnumber the amount of Major Arcana cards, you are being provided with clues regarding how you can rewrite your current story and formulate a new action plan.

Of the four suits, to which do you feel most drawn?

Of the four suits, to which do you feel least drawn?

Take a moment now and separate your deck into two piles.

In the first pile, place all of the Minor Arcana. In the second pile, place all of the Major Arcana.

Next, separate the Minor Arcana cards into the four suits and place them in numerical order: one through ten, and Page, Knight, Queen, King.

Allow yourself to look through each suit, and become acquainted with the cards. Begin noticing the different story that takes place in each suit.

Understanding the imagery of the Tarot begins with understanding your own personal associations with symbols and numbers. Once you allow spontaneous associations to flow through you, the stories will begin to emerge.

DAY 17

Cups

Today we are going to explore the suit of cups. Name three things that come to mind when you hear the word cup:

1.

2.

3.

Take a moment to close your eyes and bring to mind the image of a cup. You can drink from cups, and cups hold water; thus, the element of water is associated with the suit of cups. Water is a fluid element, one that shapes itself to the form of the vessel into which it is placed. When the cup is small, only a small amount of water can be held. The larger the cup, the more water can be held. If you try to put too much water into a small cup, it overflows.

The same can be said about the heart. A heart with a small amount of room can hold a small amount of love, and a heart with more room can hold a greater amount of love. Sometimes a heart overflows with love. Therefore, it is appropriate that the suit of Cups is associated with matters of the heart and emotions.

In the world of astrology, because cups are associated with the element of water, they are also paired with the water signs of the horoscope. The water signs in astrology are Cancer, Scorpio, and Pisces.

Cups…Emotions…
Water…Water Signs

Separate the suit of Cups from your deck and place them in numerical order as you did on Day 16. For a few moments today and tomorrow, spend time looking through the suit of Cups cards, beginning with the aces and moving through the court cards. Let the story of the cups unfold for you.

What are three things that you notice about the cards within the suit of cups?

1.

2.

3.

DAY 18

Swords

Today we are going to explore the suit of Swords. Name three things that come to mind when you hear the word sword:

1.

2.

3.

Take a moment to close your eyes and bring to mind the image of a sword. A sword is a tool used for cutting, defending, and protecting. Swords move quickly through space and, as such, are associated with the element of air.

Our thoughts, which move through our minds quickly, are like swords. They cut through our awareness and can cause us to become defensive or protective. Sometimes our thoughts cut us down, cut others down, or cut away that which is no longer necessary. The suit of swords is associated with our thought processes. Both our thoughts and swords need to be wielded with care, lest their sharpness cause harm.

In the world of astrology, because swords are associated with the element of air, they are also paired with the air signs of the horoscope. These signs are: Gemini, Libra, and Aquarius.

ACE OF SWORDS

KNIGHT OF SWORDS

FOUR OF SWORDS

THREE OF SWORDS

Swords...Air...
Thoughts...Air Signs

Separate the suit of swords from your deck and place them in numerical order. For a few moments today and tomorrow, spend time looking through the suit of sword cards, beginning with the aces and moving through the court cards. Let the story of the swords unfold for you.

What are three things that you notice about the cards within the suit of swords?

1.

2.

3.

DAY 19

Rods/Wands/Staffs

T oday we are going to explore the suit of rods/wands/staffs. Name three things that come to mind when you hear the words rod, wand or staff:

1.

2.

3.

Take a moment to close your eyes bring to mind the image of a staff. Staffs are made of wood and, before the invention of electricity, they were lit and used as torches. The fire would shed light and lead the way through the darkness.

Fire, a powerful element, is associated with the suit of rods. When fire is harnessed for good, it can be used for heat and light. When fire is left to run wild, it can blaze a path of destruction. Its light aids our vision and keeps us warm. Likewise, the suit of Rods is associated with fire, vision, passion, and forward movement.

In the world of astrology, because Rods are associated with the element of fire, they are also paired with the fire signs of the horoscope. These signs are: Aires, Leo, and Sagittarius.

Rods...Fire...Action...Passion...Fire Signs

Separate the suit of rods/wands/staffs from your deck and place them in numerical order. For a few moments today and tomorrow, spend time looking through the suit of rods/wands/staffs cards, beginning with the aces and moving through the court cards. Let the story of the rods/wands/staffs unfold for you.

What are three things that you notice about the cards within the suit of rods/wands/staffs?

1.

2.

3.

DAY 20

Pentacles/Coins

Today we are going to explore the suit of Pentacles/Coins. Name three things that come to mind when you hear the words pentacle or coin:

1.

2.

3.

Take a moment to close your eyes, and bring to mind the image of a coin. A coin is a form of currency, something that determines value in our society. Wealth, education, and career create a sense of value and security in society. These things are associated with "earthly" importance.

The symbol of a pentagram is considered by some to be a powerful symbol of "earth magic." The suit of Pentacles is associated with earth, career, educational endeavors, and finances.

In the world of astrology, because Pentacles are associated with the element of earth, they are also paired with the earth signs of the horoscope. The earth signs in astrology are: Taurus, Virgo, and Capricorn.

Pentacle...Career...
Finances...Earth Signs

Separate the suit of pentacles/coins from your deck and place them in numerical order. For a few moments today and tomorrow, spend time looking through the suit of Pentacle/Coin cards, beginning with the aces and moving through the court cards. Let the story of the pentacles/coins unfold for you.

What are three things that you notice about the cards within the suit of pentacles/coins?

1.

2.

3.

Understanding the Four Suits

Before moving forward, it is important to pause and assimilate the information of the past four days about each suit in the Minor Arcana. Review the synopsis for each suit and then have fun pondering and answering the questions that follow.

Cups

* Cups hold water.
* The element of Water is associated with the suit of Cups.
* Water is a fluid element; it shapes itself to the form of the container it is placed in.
* Small cup = small amount of water. Large cup = larger amount of water
* Put too much water into a small cup and it overflows.
* The same can be said about the heart.
* A heart with a small amount of room can hold a small amount of love.
* A heart with more room can hold more love.
* Sometimes a heart overflows with love.
* The suit of Cups is associated with matters of the heart and emotions.
* Cups are associated with water and are paired with the Water signs of the horoscope: Cancer, Scorpio, and Pisces.

Swords

* A sword is a tool used for cutting, defending, and protecting.
* Swords move quickly through the air and are associated with the element of air.
* Our thoughts, like swords, move through our minds quickly.
* Thoughts cut through our awareness.
* Our thoughts can cause us to become defensive or protective.
* Sometimes our thoughts cut us down, cut others down, or cut away that which is no longer necessary.
* The suit of Swords is associated with air and our thought processes.
* Both our thoughts and swords need to be wielded with care lest their sharpness cause harm.
* Swords are associated with the element of Air and are paired with the Air signs of the horoscope: Gemini, Libra, and Aquarius.

ACE OF CUPS

TWO OF SWORDS

THREE OF WANDS

FOUR OF PENTACLES

Rods/Wands/Staffs

- Staff's are made of wood.
- Before electricity, staffs were lit and used as torches.
- Fire from a torch sheds light and leads the way through the darkness.
- Fire is associated with the suit of Rods/Wands/Staffs and is a powerful element. It encompasses vision, passion, and forward movement
- When fire is harnessed for good, it can be used for heat and light.
- When fire is left to run wild, it can blaze a path of destruction.
- Its light aids our vision and the flames keep us warm.
- Rods are associated with the element of Fire and are paired with the Fire signs of the horoscope: Aires, Leo, and Sagittarius.

Pentacles/Coins

- A coin is a form of currency.
- Currency determines value in our society.
- Wealth, education, and career create a sense of value and security.
- Wealth, education, and career are associated with "earthly" importance.
- The symbol of a pentagram is considered by some to be a powerful symbol of "earth magic."
- The suit of Pentacles/Coins is associated with earth, career, educational endeavors, and finances.
- Pentacles and Coins are associated with the element of Earth and are paired with the Earth signs of the horoscope: Taurus, Virgo, and Capricorn.

Questions to Ponder:

1. What suit would most likely show up if a person were asking a question regarding her/his love life?

2. If someone asked a question about love and a number of swords were in the layout, what might be happening?

3. What would the characteristics of a person be if a great number of rods showed up in the layout?

4. If a great number of pentacles showed up in a reading, what matters might impact the person asking the question?

5. If someone asked a question about his or her career and the reading contained mostly Major Arcana, what could you surmise?

6. What possible issues are present when a majority of the cards show up in the following suits:

Cups:

Rods:

Swords:

Pentacles:

7. Write three adjectives that you associate with each of the elements:

Cups:

Rods:

Swords:

Pentacles:

DAY 22

Aces
(Part One)

N ow that we have an understanding of the four suits of the Minor Arcana, it is time to explore each number. We will spend two days getting to know each number individually. Hopefully by this point in your journey, the incorporation of conscious breath-work before each exercise is a well-ingrained habit.

What thoughts come to mind when you hear the words **ace** or **one**?
Take a moment and write down three thoughts:

1.

2.

3.

After teaching others and speaking with colleagues and friends over the years, I have found that there are a number of similar associations with numbers. I have created a list of associations (following). If your associations are different, it just means that you are creating new associations for your personal dream interpretation guide.

ACE OF CUPS

ACE OF SWORDS

ACE OF WANDS

ACE OF PENTACLES

Possible Associations with the Number ONE:

- Being one of a kind
- Being number one
- Creation
- The beginning or start of something
- Raw potential
- January (the first month)
- Timing: one day, one week, one month, one year

Once we have our own list of associations, we can combine that list with what we have learned about each suit in the Tarot. Choose three possible associations for the number **one**. They can be your associations, my associations, or a mixture of the two. Once you have chosen them, combine each association with each suit. Below is an example:

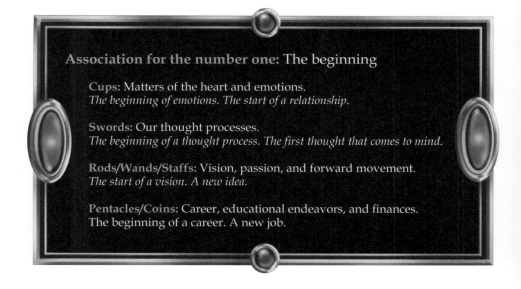

Association for the number one: The beginning

    Cups: Matters of the heart and emotions.
    The beginning of emotions. The start of a relationship.

    Swords: Our thought processes.
    The beginning of a thought process. The first thought that comes to mind.

    Rods/Wands/Staffs: Vision, passion, and forward movement.
    The start of a vision. A new idea.

    Pentacles/Coins: Career, educational endeavors, and finances.
    The beginning of a career. A new job.

Now it's your turn.

First Association:

    Cups:

    Swords:

    Rods/Wands/Staffs:

    Pentacles/Coins:

Second Association:

    Cups:

    Swords:

    Rods/Wands/Staffs:

    Pentacles/Coins:

Third Association:

    Cups:

    Swords:

    Rods/Wands/Staffs:

    Pentacles/Coins:

DAY 23

Aces
(Part Two)

Let's continue with the **aces/ones** by combining the exercises from yesterday and working directly with your own deck. Each of these exercises is designed to help you create your own personal dialogue with your deck.

Start by connecting with your breath and practicing some conscious breathing techniques.

Write down three words that you associate with the number **one**. These can be the same answers that you gave yesterday or three new ones.

1.

2.

3.

Today's Exercise

1. Separate the four **aces** from your deck.
2. Lay them out upright and in a line, taking a moment to study each card.
3. Now, turn the cards over and mix them up.
4. Pick one and look at it. Let it tell you a story.
5. Write three to five sentences about the card that you chose in the space below.
    What numbers, colors, and symbols do you notice? Bring the colors, symbol,
    and the numerology for the card together, and just allow your thoughts to flow
    as you write.
6. Do this for each of the **aces**.

   ACE of Cups:

   ACE of Swords:

   ACE of Rods:

   ACE of Pentacles:

When you begin to observe your associations with colors, numbers, and symbols, and put it together, the Tarot becomes easy to understand. Therefore, the pressure is taken out of trying to memorize the meanings of seventy-eight different cards.

DAY 24

Twos
(Part One)

What thoughts come to mind when you hear the word **two**? Take a moment and write down three of them:

1.

2.

3.

Possible Associations with the Number TWO:

- Duality / the "either one or another" comparison
- Unity
- Joining together
- Balance
- Partnership
- February (the 2nd month)
- Timing: two days, two weeks, two months, two years

Once we have our own list of associations, we can combine that list with what we have learned about each suit in the Tarot. Choose three possible associations for the number **two**. They can be your associations, my associations, or a mixture of the two. Once you have chosen them, combine each association with each suit. Look back at the example for the number **one** if you have any questions.

TWO OF CUPS

TWO OF SWORDS

TWO OF WANDS

TWO OF PENTACLES

First Association:

    Cups:

    Swords:

    Rods/Wands/Staffs:

    Pentacles/Coins:

Second Association:

    Cups:

    Swords:

    Rods/Wands/Staffs:

    Pentacles/Coins:

Third Association:

    Cups:

    Swords:

    Rods/Wands/Staffs:

    Pentacles/Coins:

DAY 25

Twos
(Part Two)

Let's continue with the **twos** by combining the exercises from yesterday and working directly with your own deck. Each of these exercises is designed to help you create your own personal dialogue with your deck.

Start by connecting with your breath and practicing some conscious breathing techniques.

Write down three words that you associate with the number **two**. These can be the same answers that you gave yesterday or three new ones.

1.

2.

3.

Today's Exercise

1. Separate the four **twos** from your deck.
2. Lay them out upright and in a line, taking a moment to study each card.
3. Now, turn them over and mix them up.
4. Pick one and look at it. Let it tell you a story.
5. Write three to five sentences about the card that you chose. What numbers, colors and symbols do you notice? Bring the colors, symbols, and the numerology for the card together and just allow your thoughts to flow as you write.
6. Do this for each of the twos.

TWO of Cups:

TWO of Swords:

TWO of Rods:

TWO of Pentacles:

DAY 26

Threes
(Part One)

W hat thoughts come to mind when you hear the word **three**? Take a moment and write down three of them:

1.

2.

3.

Possible Associations with the Number THREE:

- Creation (the union of two creates a third)
- Cycles (past, present, future)
- Triangles
- Balance
- Nurturing or giving birth
- Month of March (third month)
- Timing: three days, three weeks, three months, three years

Once we have our own list of associations, we can combine that list with what we have learned about each suit in the Tarot. Choose three possible associations for the number **three**. They can be your associations, my associations, or a mixture of the two. Once you have chosen them, combine each association with each suit. Look back at the example for the number **one** if you have any questions.

THREE OF CUPS

THREE OF SWORDS

THREE OF WANDS

THREE OF PENTACLES

First Association:

    Cups:

    Swords:

    Rods/Wands/Staffs:

    Pentacles/Coins:

Second Association:

    Cups:

    Swords:

    Rods/Wands/Staffs:

    Pentacles/Coins:

Third Association:

    Cups:

    Swords:

    Rods/Wands/Staffs:

    Pentacles/Coins:

DAY 27

Threes
(Part Two)

Let's continue with the **threes** by combining the exercises from yesterday and working directly with your own deck. Each of these exercises is designed to help you create your own personal dialogue with your deck.

Start by connecting with your breath and practicing some conscious breathing techniques.

Write down three words that you associate with the number **three**. These can be the same answers that you gave yesterday or three new ones.

1.

2.

3.

Today's Exercise

1. Separate the four **threes** from your deck.
2. Lay them out upright and in a line, taking a moment to study each card.
3. Now turn them over and mix them up.
4. Pick one and look at it. Let it tell you a story.
5. Write three to five sentences about the card that you chose. What numbers, colors, and symbols do you notice? Bring the colors, symbols and the numerology for the card together and just allow your thoughts to flow as you write.
6. Do this for each of the **threes**.

Three of Cups:

Three of Swords:

Three of Rods:

Three of Pentacles:

DAY 28

Fours
(Part One)

W hat thoughts come to mind when you hear the word **four**? Take a moment and write down three of them:

1.

2.

3.

Possible Associations with the Number FOUR:

- Stability
- Structure
- Practicality
- Foundation
- Conventionality
- Month of April (fourth month)
- Timing: four days, four weeks, four months, four years

Once we have our own list of associations, we can combine that list with what we have learned about each suit in the Tarot. Choose three possible associations for the number **four**. They can be your associations, my associations, or a mixture of the two. Once you have chosen them, combine each association with each suit. Look back at the example for the **number one** if you have any questions.

FOUR OF CUPS

FOUR OF SWORDS

FOUR OF WANDS

FOUR OF PENTACLES

First Association:

    Cups:

    Swords:

    Rods/Wands/Staffs:

    Pentacles/Coins:

Second Association:

    Cups:

    Swords:

    Rods/Wands/Staffs:

    Pentacles/Coins:

Third Association:

    Cups:

    Swords:

    Rods/Wands/Staffs:

    Pentacles/Coins:

Fours
(Part Two)

L et's continue with the **fours** by combining the exercises from yesterday and working directly with your own deck. Each of these exercises is designed to help you create your own personal dialogue with your deck.

Start by connecting with your breath and practicing some conscious breathing techniques.

Write down three words that you associate with the number **four**. These can be the same answers that you gave yesterday or three new ones.

1.

2.

3.

Today's Exercise

1. Separate the four **fours** from your deck.
2. Lay them out upright and in a line, taking a moment to study each card.
3. Now turn them over and mix them up.
4. Pick one and look at it and let it tell you a story.
5. Write three to five sentences about the card that you chose. What numbers, colors and symbols do you notice? Bring the colors, symbols and the numerology for the card together and just allow your thoughts to flow as you write.
6. Do this for each of the **fours**.

FOUR of Cups:

FOUR of Swords:

FOUR of Rods:

FOUR of Pentacles:

Fives
(Part One)

W hat thoughts come to mind when you hear the word **five**? Take a moment and write down three of them:

1.

2.

3.

Possible Associations with the Number FIVE:

- Challenge
- Restlessness
- Unpredictability
- Adventure
- Integration
- Month of May (fifth month)
- Timing: five days, five weeks, five months, five years

Once we have our own list of associations, we can combine that list with what we have learned about each suit in the Tarot. Choose three possible associations for the number **five**. They can be your associations, my associations or a mixture of the two. Once you have chosen them, combine each association with each suit. Look back at the example for the **number one** if you have any questions.

FIVE OF CUPS

FIVE OF SWORDS

FIVE OF WANDS

FIVE OF PENTACLES

First Association:

    Cups:

    Swords:

    Rods/Wands/Staffs:

    Pentacles/Coins:

Second Association:

    Cups:

    Swords:

    Rods/Wands/Staffs:

    Pentacles/Coins:

Third Association:

    Cups:

    Swords:

    Rods/Wands/Staffs:

    Pentacles/Coins:

DAY 31

Fives
(Part Two)

Let's continue with the **fives** by combining the exercises from yesterday and working directly with your own deck. Each of these exercises is designed to help you create your own personal dialogue with your deck.

Start by connecting with your breath and practicing some conscious breathing techniques.

Write down three words that you associate with the number **five**. These can be the same answers that you gave yesterday or three new ones.

1.

2.

3.

Today's Exercise

1. Separate the four **fives** from your deck.
2. Lay them out upright and in a line, taking a moment to study each card.
3. Now turn them over and mix them up.
4. Pick one and look at it and let it tell you a story.
5. Write three to five sentences about the card that you chose. What numbers, colors and symbols do you notice? Bring the colors, symbols and the numerology for the card together and just allow your thoughts to flow as you write.
6. Do this for each of the **fives**.

FIVE of Cups:

FIVE of Swords:

FIVE of Rods:

FIVE of Pentacles:

DAY 32

Sixes
(Part One)

W hat thoughts come to mind when you hear the word **six**? Take a
moment and write down three of them:

1.

2.

3.

Possible Associations with the Number SIX

- Union
- Harmony
- Equality
- Balance
- Reliability
- Month of June (sixth month)
- Timing: six days, six weeks, six months, six years

Once we have our own list of associations, we can combine that list
with what we have learned about each suit in the Tarot. Choose three
possible associations for the number **six**. They can be your associations, my
associations or a mixture of the two. Once you have chosen them, combine
each association with each suit. Look back at the example for the **number
one** if you have any questions.

SIX OF CUPS

SIX OF SWORDS

SIX OF WANDS

SIX OF PENTACLES

First Association:

   Cups:

   Swords:

   Rods/Wands/Staffs:

   Pentacles/Coins:

Second Association:

   Cups:

   Swords:

   Rods/Wands/Staffs:

   Pentacles/Coins:

Third Association:

   Cups:

   Swords:

   Rods/Wands/Staffs:

   Pentacles/Coins:

Sixes
(Part Two)

L et's continue with the **sixes** by combining the exercises from yesterday and working directly with your own deck. Each of these exercises is designed to help you create your own personal dialogue with your deck.

Start by connecting with your breath and practicing some conscious breathing techniques.

Write down three words that you associate with the number **six**. These can be the same answers that you gave yesterday or three new ones.

1.

2.

3.

Today's Exercise

1. Separate the four **sixes** from your deck.
2. Lay them out upright and in a line, taking a moment to study each card.
3. Now turn them over and mix them up.
4. Pick one and look at it and let it tell you a story.
5. Write three to five sentences about the card that you chose. What numbers, colors and symbols do you notice? Bring the colors, symbols and the numerology for the card together and just allow your thoughts to flow as you write.
6. Do this for each of the **sixes**.

SIX of Cups:

SIX of Swords:

SIX of Rods:

SIX of Pentacles:

DAY 34

Sevens
(Part One)

W hat thoughts come to mind when you hear the word **seven**? Take a moment and write down three of them:

1.

2.

3.

Possible Associations with the Number SEVEN:

- Wisdom
- Fortune
- Evolution
- Manifestation
- Progress
- Month of July (seventh month)
- Timing: seven days, seven weeks, seven months, seven years

Once we have our own list of associations, we can combine that list with what we have learned about each suit in the Tarot. Choose three possible associations for the number **seven**. They can be your associations, my associations or a mixture of the two. Once you have chosen them, combine each association with each suit. Look back at the example for the **number one** if you have any questions.

SEVEN OF CUPS

SEVEN OF SWORDS

SEVEN OF WANDS

SEVEN OF PENTACLES

First Association:

Cups:

Swords:

Rods/Wands/Staffs:

Pentacles/Coins:

Second Association:

Cups:

Swords:

Rods/Wands/Staffs:

Pentacles/Coins:

Third Association:

Cups:

Swords:

Rods/Wands/Staffs:

Pentacles/Coins:

DAY 35

Sevens
(Part Two)

L et's continue with the **sevens** by combining the exercises from yesterday and working directly with your own deck. Each of these exercises is designed to help you create your own personal dialogue with your deck.

Start by connecting with your breath and practicing some conscious breathing techniques.

Write down three words that you associate with the number **seven**. These can be the same answers that you gave yesterday or three new ones.

1.

2.

3.

Today's Exercise

1. Separate the four sevens from your deck.
2. Lay them out upright and in a line, taking a moment to study each card.
3. Now turn them over and mix them up.
4. Pick one and look at it and let it tell you a story.
5. Write three to five sentences about the card that you chose. What numbers, colors and symbols do you notice? Bring the colors, symbols and the numerology for the card together and just allow your thoughts to flow as you write.
6. Do this for each of the **sevens**.

SEVEN of Cups:

SEVEN of Swords:

SEVEN of Rods:

SEVEN of Pentacles:

DAY 36

Eights
(Part One)

W hat thoughts come to mind when you hear the word **eight**? Take a moment and write down three of them:

1.

2.

3.

Possible Associations with the Number EIGHT:

- Cycles
- Infinity
- Fluidity
- Success
- Intention
- Month of August (eighth month)
- Timing: eight days, eight weeks, eight months, eight years

Once we have our own list of associations, we can combine that list with what we have learned about each suit in the Tarot. Choose three possible associations for the number **eight**. They can be your associations, my associations or a mixture of the two. Once you have chosen them, combine each association with each suit. Look back at the example for the **number one** if you have any questions.

EIGHT OF CUPS

EIGHT OF SWORDS

EIGHT OF WANDS

EIGHT OF PENTACLES

First Association:

    Cups:

    Swords:

    Rods/Wands/Staffs:

    Pentacles/Coins:

Second Association:

    Cups:

    Swords:

    Rods/Wands/Staffs:

    Pentacles/Coins:

Third Association:

    Cups:

    Swords:

    Rods/Wands/Staffs:

    Pentacles/Coins:

Eights
(Part Two)

L et's continue with the **eights** by combining the exercises from yesterday and working directly with your own deck. Each of these exercises is designed to help you create your own personal dialogue with your deck.

Start by connecting with your breath and practicing some conscious breathing techniques.

Write down three words that you associate with the number **eight**. These can be the same answers that you gave yesterday or three new ones.

1.

2.

3.

Today's Exercise

1. Separate the four **eights** from your deck.
2. Lay them out upright and in a line, taking a moment to study each card.
3. Now turn them over and mix them up.
4. Pick one and look at it and let it tell you a story.
5. Write three to five sentences about the card that you chose. What numbers, colors and symbols do you notice? Bring the colors, symbols and the numerology for the card together and just allow your thoughts to flow as you write.
6. Do this for each of the **eights**.

EIGHT of Cups:

EIGHT of Swords:

EIGHT of Rods:

EIGHT of Pentacles:

Nines
(Part One)

What thoughts come to mind when you hear the word **nine**? Take a moment and write down three of them:

1.

2.

3.

Possible Associations with the Number NINE:

* Accomplishment
* Power
* Influence
* Completion
* Culmination
* Month of September (ninth month)
* Timing: nine days, nine weeks, nine months, nine years

Once we have our own list of associations, we can combine that list with what we have learned about each suit in the Tarot. Choose three possible associations for the number **nine**. They can be your associations, my associations or a mixture of the two. Once you have chosen them, combine each association with each suit. Look back at the example for the **number one** if you have any questions.

NINE OF CUPS

NINE OF SWORDS

NINE OF WANDS

NINE OF PENTACLES

First Association:

    Cups:

    Swords:

    Rods/Wands/Staffs:

    Pentacles/Coins:

Second Association:

    Cups:

    Swords:

    Rods/Wands/Staffs:

    Pentacles/Coins:

Third Association:

    Cups:

    Swords:

    Rods/Wands/Staffs:

    Pentacles/Coins:

DAY 39

Nines
(Part Two)

L et's continue with the **nines** by combining the exercises from yesterday and working directly with your own deck. Each of these exercises is designed to help you create your own personal dialogue with your deck.

Start by connecting with your breath and practicing some conscious breathing techniques.

Write down three words that you associate with the number **nine**. These can be the same answers that you gave yesterday or three new ones.

1.

2.

3.

Today's Exercise

1. Separate the four **nines** from your deck.
2. Lay them out upright and in a line, taking a moment to study each card.
3. Now turn them over and mix them up.
4. Pick one and look at it and let it tell you a story.
5. Write three to five sentences about the card that you chose. What numbers, colors and symbols do you notice? Bring the colors, symbols and the numerology for the card together and just allow your thoughts to flow as you write.
6. Do this for each of the **nines**.

NINE of Cups:

NINE of Swords:

NINE of Rods:

NINE of Pentacles:

Tens
(Part One)

Whathat thoughts come to mind when you hear the word **ten**? Take a moment and write down three of them:

1.

2.

3.

Possible Associations with the Number TEN:

- Completion
- Perfection
- Wholeness
- All possibilities
- Total fulfillment
- Month of October (tenth month)
- Timing: ten days, ten weeks, ten months, ten years

Once we have our own list of associations, we can combine that list with what we have learned about each suit in the Tarot. Choose three possible associations for the number **ten**. They can be your associations, my associations or a mixture of the two. Once you have chosen them, combine each association with each suit. Look back at the example I gave with the **number one** if you have any questions.

TEN OF CUPS

TEN OF SWORDS

TEN OF WANDS

TEN OF PENTACLES

First Association:

    Cups:

    Swords:

    Rods/Wands/Staffs:

    Pentacles/Coins:

Second Association:

    Cups:

    Swords:

    Rods/Wands/Staffs:

    Pentacles/Coins:

Third Association:

    Cups:

    Swords:

    Rods/Wands/Staffs:

    Pentacles/Coins:

Tens
(Part Two)

Let's continue with the **tens** by combining the exercises from yesterday and working directly with your own deck. Each of these exercises is designed to help you create your own personal dialogue with your deck.

Start by connecting with your breath and practicing some conscious breathing techniques.

Write down three words that you associate with the number **ten**. These can be the same answers that you gave yesterday or three new ones.

1.

2.

3.

Today's Exercise

1. Separate the four **tens** from your deck.
2. Lay them out upright and in a line, taking a moment to study each card.
3. Now turn them over and mix them up.
4. Pick one and look at it and let it tell you a story.
5. Write three to five sentences about the card that you chose. What numbers, colors and symbols do you notice? Bring the colors, symbols and the numerology for the card together and just allow your thoughts to flow as you write.
6. Do this for each of the **tens**.

TEN of Cups:

TEN of Swords:

TEN of Rods:

TEN of Pentacles:

DAY 42

The Court Cards

The Court Cards of the Minor Arcana each have their own story. Each suit (Cups, Rods, Swords or Pentacles) contains four court cards: the Page, Knight, Queen, and King.

In medieval times, a Page was a young helper. As such, the Page can be associated with a young person or child. Pages were also those who delivered messages. Therefore, when they show up in a reading, they can be delivering thoughts or ideas (Swords), a message of love (Cups), inspiration (Wands), or money, education, or career (Pentacles). Did this already occur to you after completing the associations for the numbers? I thought so. Recognizing your associations is the key to reading the Tarot without rote memorization of the cards.

The Knight is the next in the hierarchy of the court cards. Knights were warriors, those who rode in to save the day. They traveled from place to place based on where they were needed. They were not committed to staying-put in one place and were explorers in search of as many new kingdoms as they could find. The Knight is associated with the period of adolescence, as this is a time of movement and high drama. Like their story, the messages they bring in readings regard movement, delays (when card is reversed), trips, an arrival, or a departure.

Although the Pages and Knights were male in medieval times, today we can view them as masculine or feminine, giving them a unisex meaning. Trust your intuition, the surrounding cards and the voice of the Divine Storyteller within you to indicate whether the Knight or Page in the reading represents a female or male.

The Queen and King represent adulthood. They are the highest one can achieve in the ranking of the court cards, as they are the rulers in control of their own kingdoms.

In terms of evolution, the order from lowest to highest ranking in matters of achievement and status are: Page, Knight, and Queen/King. In terms of maturity and commitment in relationships, a Page is a friend, a Knight is a possible affair or noncommittal partner, and a Queen or King are committed to the relationship. The Queens and Kings can indicate a wife, husband, or long-term partners.

Where do you stand in your relationships? To find out, try the following exercise with your cards.

KING OF PENTACLES

PAGE OF PENTACLES

OF PENTACLES

Relationship Exercise

Separate all of the court cards from your deck and shuffle them. Think of an important relationship in your life and pull a card. You can choose to either keep each card out as you draw it or put it back in the deck before you ask about another relationship. Try asking some of these questions for fun:

1. How am I showing up in my career (or at school)?

2. How am I showing up in my intimate relationship?

3. How am I showing up in my family?

To take this exercise a step further, put all of your cards together, shuffle them again, and ask how you can bring that particular relationship to the next level (or make the relationship less committed). Draw three cards to determine whether or not to leave the details to your God source or take action (Day 15). If you are to take action, separate all of the numbered cards from your deck and shuffle them. Draw three cards and lay them out. Let them tell you a story and give you an action plan. Have fun with this, using any and all of the tools that you have learned so far as you allow the answers to flow through you.

When you begin to see how you associate the suits, colors and symbols with each court card and put everything together, the Tarot becomes easy to understand. The intention here is to help you develop a dialogue between yourself and your deck. It takes the pressure out of trying to memorize the meanings of seventy-eight different cards, doesn't it?

DAY 43

The Page
(Part One)

L et's begin our journey through the court cards of the Minor Arcana. We will spend two days with each court card, as we did with the numbers, to insure an exploration that will help your associations flow with effortless ease.

As mentioned, in medieval times, a **Page** was a young helper or someone who delivered messages. **Pages** are associated with messages or children.

What thoughts come to mind when you think of a **Page**? Take a moment and write down three of them:

1.

2.

3.

Understanding the imagery of the Tarot continues with understanding your own personal associations with the court cards.

PAGE OF CUPS

PAGE OF SWORDS

PAGE OF WANDS

PAGE OF PENTACLES

Possible Associations with the Page

- Messages
- A messenger
- Devotion
- Service
- A child/young person
- Someone lacking maturity in a relationship
- A friend
- A dreamer
- A beginner

Once we have our own list of associations, we can combine that list with what we have learned about each suit in the Tarot. Choose three possible associations for the **Page**. They can be your associations, my associations, or a mixture of the two. Once you have chosen them, combine each association with each suit. Look back at the example I gave with the **number one** if you have any questions.

First Association:

Cups:

Swords:

Rods/Wands/Staffs:

Pentacles/Coins:

Second Association:

Cups:

Swords:

Rods/Wands/Staffs:

Pentacles/Coins:

Third Association:

   Cups:

   Swords:

   Rods/Wands/Staffs:

   Pentacles/Coins:

Take a moment and remove the four **Page** cards from the deck. Shuffle them and pick one. Look at the images on the card. Based on the associations from above, what message does the card give you? Place the card where you will see it throughout the day or even on your altar (if you have one). At the end of the day, ask yourself how the meanings that you associated with your **Page** card were present in your day.

DAY 44

The Page
(Part Two)

Let's continue with the **Pages** by combining what we have learned about our understanding of the suits with the imagery on your cards. Each of these exercises is designed to help you create your own personal dialogue with your deck.

Start by separating the four **Pages** from your deck. Lay them out upright and in a line and take a moment to study the images. Notice the different symbols and images for each suit. Notice the different colors represented by each suit.

Write three to five sentences about each card. Just allow your thoughts to flow through you.

- What images/symbols are present for each suit?
- What colors are predominant?
- What story does each card tell you?

PAGE of Cups:

PAGE of Rods:

PAGE of Swords:

PAGE of Pentacles:

DAY 45

The Knight
(Part One)

A s mentioned, Knights were warriors, those who "rode in to save the day." They traveled from place to place based on where they were needed. They were not committed to staying-put in one place and were explorers in search of as many new kingdoms as they could find. The Knight is associated with the period of adolescence, as this is a time of movement and high drama. Like their story, the messages they bring in readings regard movement, delays, trips, an arrival, or a departure.

What thoughts come to mind when you think of a **Knight**? Take a moment and write down three of them:

1.

2.

3.

KNIGHT OF CUPS

KNIGHT OF SWORDS

KNIGHT OF WANDS

KNIGHT OF PENTACLES

Possible Associations with the Knight

- Movement
- Delays
- Trips
- Arrivals/departures
- An adolescent
- Someone lacking commitment in a relationship
- Vitality
- Passion
- An affair
- Impulse

Once we have our own list of associations, we can combine that list with what we have learned about each suit in the Tarot. Choose three possible associations for the **Knight**. They can be your associations, my associations, or a mixture of the two. Once you have chosen them, combine each association with each suit. Look back at the example I gave with the **number one** if you have any questions.

First Association: **Second Association:**

Cups: **Cups:**

Swords: **Swords:**

Rods/Wands/Staffs: **Rods/Wands/Staffs:**

Pentacles/Coins: **Pentacles/Coins:**

Third Association:

Cups:

Swords:

Rods/Wands/Staffs:

Pentacles/Coins:

Take a moment and remove the four **Knight** cards from the deck. Shuffle them and pick one. Look at the images on the card. Based on the associations from above, what message does the card give you? Place the card where you will see it throughout the day or even on your altar (if you have one). At the end of the day, ask yourself how the meanings that you associated with your **Knight** card were present in your day.

The Knight
(Part Two)

Let's continue with the **Knights** by combining what we have learned about our understanding of the suits with the imagery on your cards. Each of these exercises is designed to help you create your own personal dialogue with your deck.

Start by separating the four **Knights** from your deck. Lay them out upright and in a line and take a moment to study the images.

Write three to five sentences about each card. Just allow your thoughts to flow through you.

- What images/symbols are present for each suit?
- What colors are predominant?
- What story does each card tell you?

KNIGHT of Cups:

KNIGHT of Rods:

KNIGHT of Swords:

KNIGHT of Pentacles:

DAY 47

The Queen
(Part One)

The **Queen** is the female ruler of the kingdom. She is the highest female role one can achieve in the evolution of the court cards. Her feminine side helps her rule with subtlety. In relationships, a **Queen** would be someone in a committed relationship. The **Queens** can often indicate a wife or common-law spouse.

What thoughts come to mind when you think of a **Queen**? Take a moment and write down three of them:

1.

2.

3.

QUEEN OF CUPS

QUEEN OF SWORDS

QUEEN OF WANDS

QUEEN OF PENTACLES

Possible Associations with the Queen

- A Wife
- An Ex-wife (if reversed)
- Devotion
- Femininity
- A mother
- Nurturing
- Refinement
- Maturity
- Reliability

Once we have our own list of associations, we can combine that list with what we have learned about each suit in the Tarot. Choose three possible associations for the **Queen**. They can be your associations, my associations or a mixture of the two. Once you have chosen them, combine each association with each suit. Look back at the example I gave with the **number one** if you have any questions.

First Association: **Second Association:**

  Cups: **Cups:**

  Swords: **Swords:**

  Rods/Wands/Staffs: **Rods/Wands/Staffs:**

  Pentacles/Coins: **Pentacles/Coins:**

hird Association:

Cups:

Swords:

Rods/Wands/Staffs:

Pentacles/Coins:

Take a moment and remove the four **Queen** cards from the deck. Shuffle hem and pick one. Look at the images on the card. Based on the associations rom above, what message does the card give you? Place the card where ou will see it throughout the day or even on your altar (if you have one). At the end of the day, ask yourself how the meanings that you associated vith your **Queen** card were present in your day.

DAY 48

The Queen
(Part Two)

L et's continue with the **Queens** by combining what we have learned about our understanding of the suits with the imagery on your cards. Each of these exercises is designed to help you create your own personal dialogue with your deck.

Start by separating the four **Queens** from your deck. Lay them out upright and in a line and take a moment to study the images.

Write three to five sentences about each card. Just allow your thoughts to flow through you.

- What images/symbols are present for each suit?
- What colors are predominant?
- What story does each card tell you?

QUEEN of Cups:

QUEEN of Rods:

QUEEN of Swords:

QUEEN of Pentacles:

The King
(Part One)

The **King** is the male ruler of the kingdom. He is the highest male role one can achieve in the evolution of the court cards. His masculine ide helps him rule with action. In relationships, a **King** would be someone n a committed relationship. The **Kings** can often indicate a husband or ommon-law spouse.

What thoughts come to mind when you think of a **King**? Take a moment nd write down three of them:

_ .

_. .

_ .

KING OF CUPS

KING OF SWORDS

KING OF WANDS

KING OF PENTACLES

Possible Associations with the King

- A Husband
- An Ex-husband (if reversed)
- Control
- Masculinity
- A father
- Strategy
- Order
- Wisdom
- Authority

Once we have our own list of associations, we can combine that list with what we have learned about each suit in the Tarot. Choose three possible associations for the **King**. They can be your associations, my associations, or a mixture of the two. Once you have chosen them, combine each association with each suit. Look back at the example I gave with the **number one** if you have any questions.

First Association:

   Cups:

   Swords:

   Rods/Wands/Staffs:

   Pentacles/Coins:

Second Association:

   Cups:

   Swords:

   Rods/Wands/Staffs:

   Pentacles/Coins:

Third Association:

Cups:

Swords:

Rods/Wands/Staffs:

Pentacles/Coins:

Take a moment and remove the four **King** cards from the deck. Shuffle them and pick one. Look at the images on the card. Based on the associations from above, what message does the card give you? Place the card where you will see it throughout the day or even on your altar (if you have one). At the end of the day, ask yourself how the meanings that you associated with your **King** card were present in your day.

DAY 50

The King
(Part Two)

Let's continue with the **Kings** by combining what we have learned about our understanding of the suits with the imagery on your cards. Each of these exercises is designed to help you create your own personal dialogue with your deck.

Start by separating the four **Kings** from your deck. Lay them out upright and in a line and take a moment to study the images.

Write three to five sentences about each card. Just allow your thoughts to flow through you.

- What images/symbols are present for each suit?
- What colors are predominant?
- What story does each card tell you?

KING of Cups:

KING of Rods:

KING of Swords:

KING of Pentacles:

DAY 51

Holding Court

Right now, you are more than halfway done with this book and well on your way to reading the Tarot. How are you feeling? What are you thinking? Not as hard as you imagined it would be, is it? It's time to combine what you have learned about the suits and the type of court card with what you have associated with their images, colors, and symbols. Have fun when you answer the questions that follow. Feel free to look back at the information you have gathered from the previous days if you need some little hints.

PAGE OF CUPS

KNIGHT OF SWORDS

QUEEN OF WANDS

KING OF PENTACLES

1. If a client asked about a potential relationship and the person she asked about showed up as a Page, what could be the message?

2. If a Knight showed up in regards to a question regarding commitment, what could you surmise?

3. Think of a Knight as being associated with an upcoming trip. Now, based on your knowledge of the elements of each suit, where might a person be traveling when each of the suits showed up?

    Cups: **Swords:**

    Wands/Rods: **Pentacles:**

4. Based on your knowledge of the elements in each suit, name some characteristic you might equate with each of the following (think of both positive and negative traits):

Queen of Cups:

King of Cups:

Queen of Rods:

King of Rods:

Queen of Swords:

King of Swords:

Queen of Pentacles:

King of Pentacles:

DAY 52

Cycles of Life
Major Arcana

B ring out the BIG GUNS! (That's what I think of when I hear the words Major Arcana.) The Major Arcana consists of twenty-two cards numbered sequentially from zero to twenty-one. Each card has a name, and often the name is listed on it. Earlier in the book, I mentioned that when a majority of Major Arcana cards appeared in a reading, the situation was Divinely orchestrated and there was no need to do anything.

Your life is something that you co-create with God. When you connect with your God source through the Tarot, you are given an overview of the story currently taking place in your life or the life of your client.

Please take a moment and separate the Major Arcana cards from your deck. Once you have done that, arrange the cards in order from zero to twenty-one. Once they are in sequential order, make four horizontal rows. Place numbers zero to four in the first row, numbers five to ten in the second, numbers eleven to sixteen in the third and numbers seventeen to twenty-two in the fourth.

The rows that you just made with the Major Arcana illustrate a metaphorical outline for a cycle in your life. As you move through life, each choice you make takes you through this framework. Sometimes life is a struggle, and sometimes it is effortless. In this outline, the Major Arcana give insight into the evolution within your stories. This cycle represents the ongoing stages through which you pass as you live life; it can also represent the fact that each of your ideas or enterprises begins with gestation and ends in completion. I have used the example of the conception, birth, and life of a child to illustrate how each Major Arcana card plays a role in the cycle. After each action, the Major Arcana card represented in that part of the cycle is in parentheses.

A couple thinks about having a child (The Fool) and join together in sexual union (The Magician). The fetus develops an awareness of her inner environment (The Priestess).

As a child, she learns lessons of nurturing from her mother (The Empress), practicality and strategy from her father (The Emperor) and life through her family, society, and her peers' belief systems (The Hierophant).

As she grows toward adulthood, she becomes aware of her sexuality and her power of choice (The Lovers).

Through her education, she chooses a skill and sets out in a direction (The Chariot). Along the way, she learns the valuable lessons of patience, courage, and passion (Strength). Sometimes these lessons cause her to detach or go within (The Hermit), as she learns that destiny can lead her in a different direction than she originally thought (The Wheel of Fortune).

Through examination and accountability of her actions (Justice), she sacrifices (The Hanged Man), transforms (Death), and is taught the importance of flexibility and fluidity (Temperance).

She looks at her own ego and current obsessions (The Devil) and may choose to take a different approach. If she ignores the signs, an upheaval (The Tower) happens and she is reconnected to her faith and hope (The Star) again. She reflects on her own cycles and patterns (The Moon) and has a breakthrough, where clarity (The Sun) emerges. She heeds the call, embraces faith in something bigger (Judgment) and reaches her goal (The World), only to realize that the cycle continues with each new idea (The Fool) she has.

This layout is a good one for self-study. I am sharing it so that you can see how the Major Arcana cards work together to form a story of their own. Enjoy studying the Major Arcana cards that you have arranged in front of yourself. Make a list of ten or more symbols that capture your attention. After each symbol, write three words that you associate with that symbol. Continue to build on the associations that you make with the images in your deck.

1.

2.

3.

4.

5.

6.

7.

8.

9.

10.

DAY 53

Writing Your Own Bestseller

Yesterday, I mentioned that the cycle of life exercise could be used for self-study. Today, I am going to take you through that exercise so that you can gain some insight into your life. Are you ready? You will need the twenty-two cards of the Major Arcana, a piece of paper, and a pen for this exercise.

1. Think of a situation in your life around in which you would like some clarity and write it down.
2. Separate the Major Arcana cards out of your deck and shuffle them as you ponder the situation that you wrote down.
3. As you shuffle, place your energy and attention into the cards.
4. Lay out the cards face-up in three or four rows.
5. Leave them just as they are, right side up or upside down, and place them back in numerical order from zero to twenty-one.
6. Once they are in sequential order, make four horizontal rows. Place numbers zero to four in the first row, numbers five to ten in the second, numbers eleven to sixteen in the third, and numbers seventeen to twenty-two in the fourth.
7. Look at your cards and notice the cards that are upside down or reversed.
8. Upright cards indicate that this part of the cycle is flowing as it should be, while reversed cards indicate an opportunity to take a deeper look at that part of the cycle. A reversed (upside down) card offers an opportunity for growth. It may represent part of the cycle in which you are getting lost.
9. For each reversed card, consult the corresponding question(s) under the "Questions for Additional Insight" section for that card in the list that follows. For example: If the Fool card is reversed, look at the questions listed after "Question Zero (The Fool)." Embrace these parts of the cycle by exploring the questions provided. This will bring awareness and improve what is taking place in your story while helping you discover the "Aha's" that are waiting for you.
10. Write the numbers of your reversed cards down the left hand side of your piece of paper. Leave enough room in between the numbers so that you have room for writing the answer to each question.

Questions for Additional Insight

0. (The Fool) How can you embrace this idea with more childlike wonder or innocence? Are you too unfocused?

1. (The Magician) What action needs to be taken?

2. (The High Priestess) What is your intuition telling you? Are you spending too much time in your head regarding this matter?

3. (The Empress) What needs to be nurtured in this situation? Where are you clinging or nagging too much?

4. (The Emperor) How are you embracing your own power in this situation? Are you too worried about status quo? How can you be more flexible?

5. (The Hierophant) Is more knowledge or education needed? How are you deceiving yourself in regards to this situation? Are your beliefs in line with your dreams?

6. (The Lovers) What about this choice causes indecision? Is this situation for the highest and best for all of those involved?

7. (The Chariot) How is your ego getting in the way? Where is more willpower needed? Do you have a clear goal and plan of action?

8. (Strength) How can you practice more patience in regards to your goal? How can you practice more kindness and compassion toward yourself and others?

9. (The Hermit) How can you create some time for solitude and introspection? Are you retreating or withdrawing unnecessarily?

10. (Wheel of Fortune) What opportunities or possibilities are presenting themselves to you in regards to this situation?

11. (Justice) How can you be more objective in this situation?

12. (The Hanged Man) What do you need to sacrifice for this to happen? From what other perspective can you approach this situation?

13. (Death) What cycle do you need to complete before you can move forward? Are you ready to transition into a new state of beliefs for this to happen?

14. (Temperance) What needs to be done for you to create more balance or harmony in this situation?

15. (The Devil) What habit, idea or belief is preventing you from achieving this goal?

16. (The Tower) What is currently creating chaos in your life and keeping your goal at bay? What are you disillusioned about?

17. (The Star) What inspires you and helps you remain optimistic in regards to this goal?

18. (The Moon) What is creating a lack of clarity, confusion or anxiety regarding this situation? What are your unrealistic expectations?

19. (The Sun) How have you become contracted or withdrawn in regards to this goal? What will help you to regain your energy and personal power?

20. (Judgment) What do you need to forgive to make this a reality? How can you tap back into your inner calling? Around what do you need to practice acceptance?

21. (The World) How are you integrating this new situation into your life? What needs to be done so that you can create integrity within yourself to embrace accomplishment, success and the fulfillment of your goal?

DAY 54

The Fool

A s you begin your journey through the Major Arcana, you can start to piece ogether the information from previous lessons nd from your own imagination. Take a look ack through at the words you used to describe he numbers and colors, and allow each card to ell you its own story.

Each card in the Tarot deck is a story onto self. Let each one tell you its individual tale. Take me to get acquainted with your deck, and the ialogue you develop with it will be strong and lear, just like your intuition. The story is right here, waiting to be heard.

We will spend one day with each Major Arcana card. Each day, take a moment to remove hat card from your deck, and begin your exploration by answering the ollowing six questions.

oday's card: The Fool

he Fool card is signified with the number (or digit) zero.

. What do you associate with this digit?

. What comes to mind when you hear the word "fool"?

. What colors seem to be calling your attention?

4. What do the colors signify to you?

5. What symbols, objects, animals, or people do you notice?

6. What do these symbols, objects, animals, or people signify to you?

    Now sit back and look at the card in its entirety. What story is being told within the frame of the card? Take a few moments and write out the story you see in the cards. Don't over think; just write and allow the card to tell you its story.

DAY 55

The Magician

R emove the following card from your deck and begin your exploration by answering the questions below.

Today's card: **The Magician**

The Magician card is signified with the number one.

1. What do you associate with this number?

2. What comes to mind when you hear the word **"magician"**?

3. What colors seem to be calling your attention?

4. What do the colors signify to you?

5. What symbols, objects, animals, or people do you notice?

6. What do these symbols, objects, animals, or people signify to you?

Now sit back and look at the card in its entirety. What story is being told within the frame of the card? Take a few moments and write out the story you see in the cards. Don't over think; just write and allow the card to tell you its story.

DAY 56

The High Priestess

Remove the following card from your deck and begin your exploration by answering the questions below.

Today's card: The High Priestess

The High Priestess card is signified with the number two.

1. What do you associate with this number?

2. What comes to mind when you hear the words **"high priestess"**?

3. What colors seem to be calling your attention?

4. What do the colors signify to you?

5. What symbols, objects, animals, or people do you notice?

6. What do these symbols, objects, animals, or people signify to you?

Now sit back and look at the card in its entirety. What story is being told within the frame of the card? Take a few moments and write out the story you see in the cards. Don't over think; just write and allow the card to tell you its story.

DAY 57

The Empress

R emove the following card from your deck and begin your exploration by answering e questions below.

oday's card: **The Empress**

he **Empress** card is signified
ith the number three.

What do you associate with this number?

What comes to mind when you hear the word
"empress"?

. What colors seem to be calling your attention?

. What do the colors signify to you?

. What symbols, objects, animals, or people do you notice?

. What do these symbols, objects, animals, or people signify to you?

Now sit back and look at the card in its entirety. What story is being told within the frame of the card? Take a few moments and write out the story you see in the cards. Don't over think; just write and allow the card to tell you its story.

DAY 58

The Emperor

Remove the following card from your deck and begin your exploration by answering the questions below.

Today's card: The Emperor

The Emperor card is signified with the number four.

1. What do you associate with this number?

2. What comes to mind when you hear the word "**emperor**"?

3. What colors seem to be calling your attention?

4. What do the colors signify to you?

5. What symbols, objects, animals, or people do you notice?

6. What do these symbols, objects, animals, or people signify to you?

Now sit back and look at the card in its entirety. What story is being told within the frame of the card? Take a few moments and write out the story you see in the cards. Don't over think; just write and allow the card to tell you its story.

The Hierophant

Remove the following card from your deck and begin your exploration by answering the questions below.

Today's card: **The Hierophant**

The Hierophant card is signified with the number five.

1. What do you associate with this number?

2. What comes to mind when you hear the words **"hierophant/pope"**?

3. What colors seem to be calling your attention?

4. What do the colors signify to you?

5. What symbols, objects, animals, or people do you notice?

6. What do these symbols, objects, animals, or people signify to you?

Now sit back and look at the card in its entirety. What story is being told within the frame of the card? Take a few moments and write out the story you see in the cards. Don't over think; just write and allow the card to tell you its story.

DAY 60
The Lovers

Remove the following card from your deck and begin your exploration by answering the questions below.

Today's card: The Lovers

The Lovers card is signified with the number six.

1. What do you associate with this number?

2. What comes to mind when you hear the word **"lovers"**?

3. What colors seem to be calling your attention?

4. What do the colors signify to you?

5. What symbols, objects, animals, or people do you notice?

6. What do these symbols, objects, animals, or people signify to you?

Now sit back and look at the card in its entirety. What story is being told within the frame of the card? Take a few moments and write out the story you see in the cards. Don't over think; just write and allow the card to tell you its story.

The Chariot

R emove the following card from your deck and begin your exploration by answering he questions below.

'oday's card: **The Chariot**

he Chariot card is signified ith the number seven.

What do you associate with this number?

What comes to mind when you hear the word "**chariot**"?

What colors seem to be calling your attention?

What do the colors signify to you?

What symbols, objects, animals, or people do you notice?

What do these symbols, objects, animals, or people signify to you?

Now sit back and look at the card in its entirety. What story is being told within the frame of the card? Take a few moments and write out the story you see in the cards. Don't over think; just write and allow the card to tell you its story.

DAY 62

Strength

R emove the following card from your deck
and begin your exploration by answering
e questions below.

oday's card: **Strength**

e **Strength** card is signified
th the number eight.

What do you associate with this number?

What comes to mind when you hear the word
"**strength**"?

What colors seem to be calling your attention?

What do the colors signify to you?

What symbols, objects, animals, or people do you notice?

What do these symbols, objects, animals, or people signify to you?

Now sit back and look at the card in its entirety. What story is being told within the frame of the card? Take a few moments and write out the story you see in the cards. Don't over think; just write and allow the card to tell you its story.

The Hermit

Remove the following card from your deck and begin your exploration by answering he questions below.

Today's card: The Hermit

The Hermit card is signified vith the number nine.

- What do you associate with this number?

- What comes to mind when you hear the word "**hermit**"?

- What colors seem to be calling your attention?

- What do the colors signify to you?

- What symbols, objects, animals, or people do you notice?

- What do these symbols, objects, animals, or people signify to you?

Now sit back and look at the card in its entirety. What story is bein; told within the frame of the card? Take a few moments and write out th story you see in the cards. Don't over think; just write and allow the car to tell you its story.

DAY 64

The Wheel of Fortune

R emove the following card from your deck and begin your exploration by answering the questions below.

Today's card: **The Wheel of Fortune**

The Wheel of Fortune card is signified with the number ten.

> *For double-digit numbers, we will look at the sum of the two digits added together.
> The sum of the two digits of the number 10 is 1 + 0, which is 1.

1. What do you associate with this number?

2. What comes to mind when you hear the term "**wheel of fortune**"?

3. What colors seem to be calling your attention?

4. What do the colors signify to you?

5. What symbols, objects, animals, or people do you notice?

6. What do these symbols, objects, animals, or people signify to you?

Now sit back and look at the card in its entirety. What story is being told within the frame of the card? Take a few moments and write out the story you see in the cards. Don't over think; just write and allow the card to tell you its story.

DAY 65
Justice

Remove the following card from your deck and begin your exploration by answering the questions below.

Today's card: **Justice**

The **Justice** card is signified with the number eleven.

> *For double-digit numbers, we will look at the sum of the two digits added together.
> The sum of the two digits of the number 11 is 1 + 1, which is 2.

. What do you associate with this number?

. What comes to mind when you hear the word **"justice"**?

. What colors seem to be calling your attention?

. What do the colors signify to you?

. What symbols, objects, animals, or people do you notice?

. What do these symbols, objects, animals, or people signify to you?

Now sit back and look at the card in its entirety. What story is being told within the frame of the card? Take a few moments and write out the story you see in the cards. Don't over think; just write and allow the card to tell you its story.

DAY 66

The Hanging Man

R emove the following card from your deck and begin your exploration by answering e questions below.

oday's card: **The Hanging Man**

he Hanging Man card is signified ith the number Twelve.

*For double-digit numbers, we will look at the sum of the two digits added together. The sum of the two digits of the number 12 is 1 + 2, which is 3.

What do you associate with this number?

What comes to mind when you hear the words "**hanging man**"?

What colors seem to be calling your attention?

What do the colors signify to you?

What symbols, objects, animals, or people do you notice?

What do these symbols, objects, animals, or people signify to you?

Now sit back and look at the card in its entirety. What story is being told within the frame of the card? Take a few moments and write out the story you see in the cards. Don't over think; just write and allow the card to tell you its story.

DAY 67

Death

Remove the following card from your deck and begin your exploration by answering he questions below.

Today's card: **Death**

he **Death** card is signified vith the number thirteen.

> *For double-digit numbers, we will look at the sum of the two digits added together. The sum of the two digits of the number 13 is 1 + 3, which is 4.

. What do you associate with this number?

. What comes to mind when you hear the word "**death**"?

. What colors seem to be calling your attention?

. What do the colors signify to you?

. What symbols, objects, animals, or people do you notice?

. What do these symbols, objects, animals, or people signify to you?

Now sit back and look at the card in its entirety. What story is bein, told within the frame of the card? Take a few moments and write out th story you see in the cards. Don't over think; just write and allow the car to tell you its story.

DAY 68

Temperance

Remove the following card from your deck and begin your exploration by answering he questions below.

oday's card: **Temperance**

he **Temperance** card is signified ith the number fourteen.

> *For double-digit numbers, we will look at the sum of the two digits added together. The sum of the two digits of the number 14 is 1 + 4, which is 5.

. What do you associate with this number?

. What comes to mind when you hear the word **"temperance"**?

. What colors seem to be calling your attention?

. What do the colors signify to you?

. What symbols, objects, animals, or people do you notice?

. What do these symbols, objects, animals, or people signify to you?

Now sit back and look at the card in its entirety. What story is being told within the frame of the card? Take a few moments and write out the story you see in the cards. Don't over think; just write and allow the card to tell you its story.

The Devil

R emove the following card from your deck and begin your exploration by answering the questions below.

Today's card: **The Devil**

The Devil card is signified with the number fifteen.

> *For double-digit numbers, we will look at the sum of the two digits added together.
> The sum of the two digits of the number 15 is 1 + 5, which is 6.

1. What do you associate with this number?

2. What comes to mind when you hear the word "**devil**"?

3. What colors seem to be calling your attention?

4. What do the colors signify to you?

5. What symbols, objects, animals, or people do you notice?

6. What do these symbols, objects, animals, or people signify to you?

Now sit back and look at the card in its entirety. What story is bein told within the frame of the card? Take a few moments and write out th story you see in the cards. Don't over think; just write and allow the car to tell you its story.

DAY 70

The Tower

R emove the following card from your deck and begin your exploration by answering the questions below.

Today's card: The Tower

The Tower card is signified with the number sixteen.

> *For double-digit numbers, we will look at the sum of the two digits added together.
> The sum of the two digits of the number 16 is 1 + 6, which is 7.

1. What do you associate with this number?

2. What comes to mind when you hear the word **"tower"**?

3. What colors seem to be calling your attention?

. What do the colors signify to you?

. What symbols, objects, animals, or people do you notice?

. What do these symbols, objects, animals, or people signify to you?

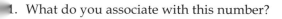

Now sit back and look at the card in its entirety. What story is being told within the frame of the card? Take a few moments and write out the story you see in the cards. Don't over think; just write and allow the card to tell you its story.

DAY 71

The Star

R emove the following card from your deck and begin your exploration by answering the questions below.

Today's card: The Star

The Star card is signified
with the number seventeen.

> *For double-digit numbers, we will look at
> the sum of the two digits added together.
>   The sum of the two digits of the number
> 17 is 1 + 7, which is 8.

THE STAR

1. What do you associate with this number?

2. What comes to mind when you hear the word "**star**"?

3. What colors seem to be calling your attention?

4. What do the colors signify to you?

5. What symbols, objects, animals, or people do you notice?

. What do these symbols, objects, animals, or people signify to you?

Now sit back and look at the card in its entirety. What story is being told within the frame of the card? Take a few moments and write out the story you see in the cards. Don't over think; just write and allow the card to tell you its story.

DAY 72

The Moon

R emove the following card from your deck
and begin your exploration by answering
he questions below.

oday's card: The Moon

he Moon card is signified
vith the number eighteen.

> *For double-digit numbers, we will look at
> the sum of the two digits added together.
> The sum of the two digits of the number
> 18 is 1 + 8, which is 9.

. What do you associate with this number?

. What comes to mind when you hear the word "**moon**"?

. What colors seem to be calling your attention?

. What do the colors signify to you?

. What symbols, objects, animals, or people do you notice?

. What do these symbols, objects, animals, or people signify to you?

Now sit back and look at the card in its entirety. What story is being told within the frame of the card? Take a few moments and write out the story you see in the cards. Don't over think; just write and allow the card to tell you its story.

The Sun

R emove the following card from your deck
and begin your exploration by answering
e questions below.

oday's card: **The Sun**

he Sun card is signified
ith the number nineteen.

> *For double-digit numbers, we will look at
> the sum of the two digits added together.
> The sum of the two digits of the number
> 19 is 1 + 9, which is 10.

What do you associate with this number?

What comes to mind when you hear the word "**sun**"?

What colors seem to be calling your attention?

What do the colors signify to you?

What symbols, objects, animals, or people do you notice?

What do these symbols, objects, animals, or people signify to you?

    Now sit back and look at the card in its entirety. What story is being told within the frame of the card? Take a few moments and write out the story you see in the cards. Don't over think; just write and allow the card to tell you its story.

DAY 74

Judgment

Remove the following card from your deck and begin your exploration by answering the questions below.

Today's card: **Judgment**

The **Judgment** card is signified with the number twenty.

*For double-digit numbers, we will look at the sum of the two digits added together.
The sum of the two digits of the number 20 is 2 + 0, which is 2.

1. What do you associate with this number?

2. What comes to mind when you hear the word "**judgment**"?

3. What colors seem to be calling your attention?

4. What do the colors signify to you?

5. What symbols, objects, animals, or people do you notice?

6. What do these symbols, objects, animals, or people signify to you?

Now sit back and look at the card in its entirety. What story is being told within the frame of the card? Take a few moments and write out the story you see in the cards. Don't over think; just write and allow the card to tell you its story.

DAY 75

The World

R emove the following card from your deck and begin your exploration by answering he questions below.

oday's card: **The World**

he World card is signified ith the number twenty-one.

> *For double-digit numbers, we will look at the sum of the two digits added together.
> The sum of the two digits of the number 21 is 2 + 1, which is 3.

What do you associate with this number?

What comes to mind when you hear the word "**world**"?

What colors seem to be calling your attention?

What do the colors signify to you?

What symbols, objects, animals, or people do you notice?

What do these symbols, objects, animals, or people signify to you?

   Now sit back and look at the card in its entirety. What story is beir
told within the frame of the card? Take a few moments and write out th
story you see in the cards. Don't over think; just write and allow the ca
to tell you its story.

SECTION THREE

Sharing the Messages You Receive

DAY 76
The Five-Second Drill

Yay! You did it! You have now established communication and connection between God (The Divine Storyteller), your entire deck, and yourself. As we move into Part Three, it's time to bring all of your tools together, so that you can begin giving readings with your 78 vignettes. Take a moment and congratulate yourself on completing Sections One and Two of this journey. You have come a long way since Day 1.

The purpose of this next exercise is to loosen up your analytical mind and shake up your inner critic, judge, and perfectionist. This is where the "fear of being wrong" may try to sneak in. Connect to your God source and allow yourself to be a conduit through which Divine messages can flow. The more you face this fear, the easier it will be to recognize your apprehension in the future. With more practice, you will become aware of the critical voice before it traps you into believing that limiting beliefs and constrictive themes are unconquerable.

The Five-Second Drill Exercise

This exercise will take you on a journey through your deck. You will look through your entire deck and spend time with all seventy-eight cards. As the title suggests, the only rule is that you spend five seconds with each card. Read through the directions once before beginning the exercise.

1. Start by shuffling the deck.
2. Close your eyes and take three deep breaths while you shuffle. This will help you connect with your deck.
3. When you are ready, stop shuffling, turn over the top card and look at it.
4. As you look at the card, say the first word that comes to your mind. (Remember, there are no right or wrong answers.) You may say anything from a color or a number to a random thought, noun, verb, name, etc. Whatever comes up is perfect.
5. Turn over the next card and repeat the actions of number 4.
6. Continue this pattern until you have gone through each card in your deck.
7. Move through the deck quickly. If no ideas come through, move to the next card, creating a pile of the "blank" cards, so that you can explore them later.

Reminder: Only spend five seconds or less on each card.

The more that you practice this exercise, the easier you will move through future readings seamlessly, thus allowing the Divine to speak through you without hesitation. This exercise helps you practice creating a quicker pathway through which the story can travel. It is an opportunity to experience being in the flow.

If you notice that you are repeating the same word for more than three cards, ask yourself: "Is this word showing up because I need to pay attention to it? Or, am I repeating myself because it is a safer action than letting my mind and intuition go?"

This is a great exercise to do with a partner because it keeps you honest with the "five second rule," and you can take turns going through the deck. To make it more fun, you can silently think of a question beforehand and listen to the words that your partner comes up with. How do these words apply to your situation?

Now you are truly connecting with your deck and developing your own personal rhythm with it. Connecting with your deck is an essential step in reading the Tarot, as it allows you to create an organic connection for reading cards. All the information that you need is already within you. The connection to the Divine has been and always will be there for you to access. This exercise is just a reminder of how you get there again.

Know that you are thoroughly prepared for this exercise. You understand the difference between the Major and Minor Arcana, as well as the stories behind them. This knowledge helps support you when you are giving a reading. You know the elements represented by each suit, and when you combine these points with your intuition while connecting to your God source, you have a winning combination.

Trust your knowledge and intuition, and let the Divine speak through you. When you open more to your God source, you will begin to see the themes within the story of your life or someone else's. The cards and the Divine will allow you to see which themes are supportive and which are constrictive.

Today practice the Five-second drill *three or four times.*

A Personal Reading for Yourself

Today you will focus on giving yourself a reading. Personal readings are the best way to practice stepping out of the way and allowing the Divine to move through you. Your ego will want to read the cards in a different way because it is attached to the outcome, but the ability to give yourself a reading is the highest form of stepping out of the way. If you can master this, you will have no problem reading for others. One of the tricks is to pretend that you are reading for someone else. Speak out loud as though another person is sitting across from you, and record the reading. This is what I do if I am looking for some Divine Guidance.

Part One

Basic Questions to Consider
When Looking at Your Cards

Pick up your deck and begin shuffling. As you shuffle, think of a question situation around which you would like some clarity. When you are ready, pull a random card from your deck. Take a few moments to answer the following questions:

1. What colors stand out to you?

2. Do any numbers grab your attention?

3. Do you notice a person or an animal on the card?

4. What action or story is being shown on the card?

5. What is the overall feeling being represented in the card? Do the actions in the card have a feeling of calmness? Happiness? Sadness? Anger?

Take a few moments and allow the story to speak to you. Pick up your pen and just allow the story or your observations to flow through you.

Part Two

Now, put the card from Part One back into your deck and shuffle the cards. Ask the Divine Storyteller what you most need to know for the day. When you are done shuffling, pick three cards and lay them out side by side. Answer the same questions from Part One and let the three cards that you just chose tell you a story. Pick up your pen and write. Don't think, just write. For fun, review your notes at the end of the day.

DAY 78

Giving Readings to Others

A Three-Part Process

Giving a reading is a multi-layered process, where each part is as beautiful as the next. The three distinct stages are: **connection, communication, and clearing**. Each stage is crucial to creating the optimum environment for your client. The following brief synopsis explains what happens during each part of the process.

Connection happens at the beginning of the reading as you connect with the Divine and with your client.

Communication happens when you open yourself to receive the messages from the Divine and share those messages with your client.

Clearing occurs after the reading is complete and helps you energetically close the connection between you, your client, and the session that you provided.

During the next eight days, you will explore these three stages in depth.
ay, we will focus on connection, which is the beginning stage of giving
ading. It is a two-part process. During the first part, you connect to your
d source by using the tools that you have learned up to this point. Only
e you have done this are you are ready for the second part, which is
ning a connection with your client.

Becoming a conduit for the Divine allows you to be a clear channel, and
 clarity happens when you are grounded. This is why it is important
pend some time prior to a reading connecting with your God source.
ether this includes meditating, taking a few deep breaths, going for a
k, or just sitting quietly as you listen to the sounds of nature, allow some
e for Divine connection.

A meditative state of mind facilitates the awareness of being fully present.
s state slows the activity of your brain and creates an alpha state, which
ites more clarity in your mind. Since your intention is to be a conduit for
r client, the ability to gain clarity is important for this to occur.

The moment that your client arrives, Part Two of the connection process
ins. As you greet your client, you can practice the conscious breathing
rcise learned at the beginning of this book. By doing this, your client now
omes your meditation. This is the key to creating a safe space for her/
. The following exercise shows you how to do just that.

Making a Person
Your Meditation Exercise

This exercise allows you to experience a greater awareness in the listening
cess. As you practice this exercise, start to notice the way that people
ond to this type of listening. This exercise creates a feeling of safety and
eptance and allows the person to experience a deeper emotional space
n the type of listening we do on an everyday basis. Do not be surprised
eople sometimes grow emotional or tear up when you listen to them
 this. Their response is a subconscious response to finally being heard.

As your friend or family member shares their story with you, give that person
our full attention.
ocus solely on the person's words.
As you inhale and exhale, imagine that you are breathing the words in and out.
Engage in soft eye contact (don't stare intently or intensely) with a pleasant,
varm look on your face.
Listen from your heart.
As the person speaks, breathe deeply in and out through your nose.
Take the breath all the way down to your belly.

8. Breathe this way the entire time the person is sharing.
9. Avoid nodding or making noises of agreement/disagreement while your partner is speaking, unless s/he stops and waits for a response.
10. When the person asks you for a response, allow the words to flow through you as you connect with the Divine.
    Respond from this space with Divine connection.
11. Keep your attention on your partner's words.
12. Allow the words to flow through you like a current flowing through a wire; when you do this, you are responding from a space free from your filters. This helps to create a feeling of safety for the person who is sharing. Often, this type of space facilitates a breakthrough for that person.

   Practice this exercise today when a friend or family member expresse frustration over a situation, and see what happens. If you are practicing thi while talking on the phone, you can still make the person your focus. To de this, you will have to be solely focused on the conversation and not trying to multi-task. The key is to find a space to sit still and absorb the person' words as s/he speaks.

DAY 79

Becoming the Conduit

onnection prepares us for communicating the messages from the
Divine. Each stage (connection, communication, clearing) builds upon
ıe next. It is important to establish your own ritual for opening yourself up
; a Divine conduit before giving a reading. Yesterday, you experienced the
ıpact that meditative listening can have in the creation of a safe, nurturing
ıvironment for your clients, friends, or family. A ritual for opening up to
ıe messages of the Divine will also create a similar environment for you
; a reader.

There are three important factors to establish your ritual:

The way you ground yourself before the session.
The connection you make with your clients as they arrive.
The prayer of intention you offer as the cards are being shuffled and before you
begin the reading.

We've explored the first two factors. Today, we will combine them
ʋith the third so that you can complete your personal preparation to be the
ɔnduit through which Divine information flows. I am sharing my ritual
; an example so that you can see the flow. Feel free to use it, or make up
variation of your own. I follow this ritual each time I work with a client.

Ideally, my ritual begins by sitting quietly for five to ten minutes before a
ıssion. If I am pressed for time, I practice the breath-work from the conscious
reathing exercises described earlier in this book. If I am giving readings
t an event or for a group of people, I use breath-work between each client.
he moment my client arrives, that person becomes my meditation, and
ıy only purpose is to serve and support her/him by being a channel for
ıe Divine. Once the client is seated across from me, I hand over the deck
ɪd ask that person to shuffle. While the client shuffles, I take a moment to
ffer a prayer of intention for the reading. While I am shuffling, I ask them
ɔ close their eyes and start taking several nice deep breaths.

For Skype or Face Time readings, I connect with them, say "hello," and
ɪen point my webcam at my hands and begin to shuffle the deck. I instruct
ıe client to take several deep breaths and let me know when it feels as
ıough I have shuffled enough. While I am shuffling I take a moment to
ffer a prayer of intention for the reading.

For phone readings, I call my client and greet her/him. I let the client
ɪow that I am beginning to shuffle the Tarot deck and will continue to do
ɔ until s/he asks ask me to stop. While I am shuffling, I take a moment and
ffer a prayer of intention for the reading.

Prayer of Intention

Masters, teachers and guides, allow my ego and I to step aside and be a clear channel to receive and share the messages for (*insert name here*) from her/his masters, teachers, and guides. I ask that the messages be for the highest and best for all involved all in the name of love. Thank you.

Completing this ritual of grounding, greeting, and offering a prayer of intention establishes my connection. Only then am I ready to communicate the messages from the Divine Storyteller. Take a moment and think about what you would like your ritual to be and write it out in the following exercise.

Creating a Ritual
for Connecting Exercise

You will need your journal and a pen. Read and complete the following sentences.

1. I ground myself by...

2. I picture greeting my client...

3. My prayer of intention is...

DAY 80

No Advice Necessary

The readings you give are meant to come from the Divine, a source that is unbiased, unfiltered, and unattached. The person with whom you work is your meditation. That person's story is meant to flow through you. If, during a reading, you find yourself beginning to give your client advice, STOP! The person sitting across from you is not *you*.

When you give advice from *your* perspective, you merely exchange one set of limiting beliefs/themes (yours) with another (the client's). When you listen to someone share her/his story, listen from a Divine space free from your filters. Breathe the person's words in and out without judgment. When the person finishe sharing and is waiting for a response, allow yourself to reconnect to your Divir Storyteller by practicing the *Making a Person Your Meditation* **Exercise** (Day 78

Once you feel connected again, allow the answers to come from that qui space of present-moment awareness. Allow the words that come from yo to take shape in that moment rather than listening, judging, and waiting fc the person's words to stop flowing so that you can speak. When you do thi then you allow words to come from the Divine rather than a space of yoι judgment, comparison, or advice. If you do feel led to interrupt the word because you are being guided by the Divine, then allow yourself to do tha

Creating an environment that facilitates a feeling of safety so that anothe person can go deeper and explore her/his own personal blockages is calle "holding space." You hold a space of unconditional love that is free from judgment. It is a way of listening at a deeper level.

Often we listen "with one ear" because our thoughts and minds are not present and fully open to the person who is talking to us. Sometimes when we do listen, we anxiously wait to share our next thought because the person's words have reminded our ego that it is past time for us to share something important. We eagerly await our next chance to be the center of attention. When we listen like this, it's a wonder that we understand one another at all.

When the other person is your meditation, your mind becomes quiet. This is one of the greatest gifts you can give to another person. "Holding space" allows someone to reach a depth one might not otherwise experience if that person was being bombarded by questions or someone's opinion.

Tapping into the Divine and listening from a space of unconditional love creates a feeling of intimacy between you and your client. Sometimes a person feels like s/he has been seen, heard, or understood for the first time in a long time. As the person offers you the sacred gift of trust, you, in exchange, may offer someone the experience of having space held the first time. How amazing is that?

The rapport a client feels with you may allow her/him to release stored emotions of which s/he was not aware. This often shows up in the form of tears. When this happens, sit quietly and allow the person to go through her/his own process. Our first instinct when someone cries is often to offer a tissue, which subconsciously tells the person to stop crying. Instead, allow your client to emote. Keep a box of tissues nearby and within eyesight, and allow the person to reach for tissues as needed. There is no need to try to make the person feel better. When you allow a person to emote in this way, you are allowing her/him to release a long-held blockage, which releases these emotions and helps the person to feel better.

Listening to another is just that: listening. The intention as a reader is to help your client step outside of her/his story and see the lessons, as well as the opportunities for growth, that are being presented. Guide the person back to looking for the lesson behind the events that take place in her/his story.

Today, notice how many times your ego anxiously waits to speak and be heard when you are talking with other people.

DAY 81

The Initial Layout
(Part One)

After you have connected to your client and the Divine, the Divine steps in and begins communicating the messages through you. As you lay out the cards, a story will begin to unfold. Allow the story to flow through you and simply speak it. The story may begin to form while you shuffle your deck or as you lay out the cards. Over the next two days, we will work with a Celtic Cross layout. Although the following layout looks like a standard Celtic Cross, I read mine a bit differently. Try out the meanings that I use with the below diagram and enjoy the flow.

Begin the reading by shuffling the cards as you say a prayer of intention for yourself and lay out a basic Celtic Cross Spread (see following diagram). Once the cards are down, look at the corresponding number for the card meaning and then write down the name of the card that you have placed there. You can choose to note whether or not it is upright or reversed.

A Note About Reversed Cards

Let me take a moment here and talk about upright cards and reversed (upside down) cards. A reversed card generally comes through with the same meaning as an upright card, but the meaning is "blocked." For example, if the Ace of Wands was upright, it could mean a surge in creativity, whereas the same card reversed could mean blocked creativity. If you get a reversed card and start to think too much about it, take a few deep breaths, connect to the Divine and allow the messages to flow through you again. Above all, I defer to my connection to the Divine and allow the message to come.

The Celtic Cross Layout

Card One:

The situation that the client currently experiences.

My Card:

Card Two:

The theme that either helps or hinders the situation.

My Card:

Card Three:

An event, feeling, thought, or experience that led to Card Four.

My Card:

Card Four:

What is being let go of because of Card Three.

My Card:

Card Five:

A new possibility about to enter one's life.

My Card:

ard Six:

What may happen as a result of Card Five.

My Card:

Card Seven:

The client's current standing or state of mind.

My Card:

Card Eight:

The outer environment, people, places, or things that affect the client.

My Card:

Card Nine:

Possible hopes and fears of the client.

My Card:

Card Ten:

The outcome based on the client's current theme.

My Card:

Also, try reading cards seven through ten together
a sentence and see what happens.

Take five to ten minutes and write down the messages that are flowing through you as you look at each card and it's corresponding meaning. Write without thinking and enjoy what is coming through you.

DAY 82

The Initial Layout
(Part Two)

The Celtic Cross Spread is useful because this initial reading gets to the heart of the stories and themes in which your client currently lives. Sometimes you may feel led to lay a few more cards down around the Celtic Cross layout to gain a clearer picture of the story. Let your intuition and the Divine guide you through this.

Today we are adding another piece to the initial Celtic Cross Spread. Begin by shuffling the cards, saying a prayer of intention for yourself, and laying out another basic Celtic Cross Spread. Once again, look at the corresponding number for the card meaning and then write down the name of the card that you have placed there. Take five to ten minutes this time and write down the messages as they come through you.

Card One:
    The situation that the client currently experiences.

    My Card:

Card Two:
    The theme that either helps or hinders the situation.

    My Card:

Card Three:

An event, feeling, thought, or experience that led to Card Four.

My Card:

Card Four:

What is being let go of because of Card Three.

My Card:

Card Five:

A new possibility about to enter one's life.

My Card:

Card Six:

What may happen as a result of Card Five.

My Card:

*Card Seven:

The client's current standing or state of mind.

My Card:

Card Eight:

The outer environment, people, places, or things that affect the client.

My Card:

Card Nine:

Possible hopes and fears of the client.

My Card:

Card Ten:

The outcome based on the client's current theme.

My Card:

Also, try reading cards seven through ten together a sentence and see what happens.

Now that you are finished reading the Celtic Cross Spread, shift into a continuous *Five-Second Drill* (Day 76) as you move through the rest of the deck, which is still in your hands. As you go through the cards, cut the deck wherever you feel led to and lay the cards down or just go through them one by one as you did in the *Five-Second Drill*. Allow yourself to lay the cards down on top of your original Celtic Cross Spread. Lay them down randomly, wherever you feel led to. It will begin to look like a giant mosaic like of images.

If your attention is drawn to a particular card in the Celtic Cross, breathe in and see what details catch your eye. Once you have reached the end of the deck and you are not holding any more cards, it is time to allow your client to ask questions. Communicate to your client that you have made your way through the deck and let her/him know that it is now time to ask any questions that s/he may have. By running through the deck first and having client receive information before s/he shares any of her/his questions or concerns, you allow the client's current story to unfold organically with all the themes intact.

DAY 83

When the Real Magic Begins

As the person's stories, patterns, and themes are presented, s/h becomes an observer in her/his own current story. This presentatic creates the space for personal breakthroughs. It is in this space that the perso receiving the reading can create the building blocks to rewrite or edit her his current story. This is the true magic that occurs during a reading.

Several things can happen once you have finished with the initial readin

- The client may want to ask questions.
- The client may want to share more of her/his story with you.
- The client may need to a few moments to absorb and process the information that has been presented.
- The client may feel complete with all of the information you have shared and have no more questions.

Even with repeat clients, each reading is a unique and differer experience.

When the client begins to ask questions, s/he may want clarification regards to something you shared in the initial reading or questions related another area of life about which s/he wants you to address. Truly listen to the client as s/he begins to ask questions. Remember the **Making a Client You Meditation Exercise** and allow the Divine to flow through you. Sometim you may see, hear, know, or feel the answers immediately without needir the cards, and sometimes you will feel led to pick up the deck, re-shuff and lay out more cards to further develop the story.

The Way a Client Shares

As you listen to your client, you extend an invitation for that person share what is going on inside. There are two ways a client will share stori with you. The client will either share by "dumping" or by "processing These are two distinctly different ways of sharing with two distinct different energies. It is important to know that if a client begins and en with "dumping," that person will remain stuck in her/his theme. When th client "processes," there is an opportunity for change.

When one is dumping, that person is trapped in the emotions or dram of her/his own story and continually looks for the next new person c which to dump the story. Rationally, the person believes that sharing he his woes and placing blame outside of the self will make her/him feel bette It is as though sharing the story again (and again and again…) will prov that the person is the victim of some cruel fate. What the person wants for someone to take her/his side, without realizing that retelling the sto actually reiterates it. The person has made her/himself into a victim t repeating the story and reinforcing the old theme. To change the curre theme, the person needs to take personal responsibility for the creation her/his themes.

I admit that there are times when I become a dumper. When this happer God has a humorous way of reminding me of what I am doing. When I a all wound up, ready to dump, and I pick up the phone, my timing is o and I reach someone's voicemail. When I shift my energy and want to ta to someone so that I can process my emotions, my friends are there ar available to talk.

You may find yourself continuing to give readings for a client wr often dumps the blame or responsibility of her/his situation on an outsic source. When this happens, listen and silently ask your God source to ser compassionate messages or questions through you to help the person becom unstuck. The role of a reader is to support the client in living the best life s he can by leading the person back to her/his God source and a story th is full of love and possibility. Sometimes, though, the client may choose remain stuck. Allow that person the choice without judging her/him for i

There is a significant energetic difference between dumping and processin When one is processing, s/he can view the situations from the point of beir an observer. The person looks at what is happening in her/his life and wh has been created by personal actions. The person takes responsibility for wh will happen as s/he moves forward and realizes that dumping keeps the se trapped in an old, outdated theme. The person is ready to move into a new or by taking the action(s) necessary to accomplish this.

Today, as you are engaged in conversation with others, notice th energetic difference you feel by someone who dumps versus someor who processes. Practice some breath-work and silently ask the Divine t guide you to be compassionate in that moment. You may feel led to say few words, ask a question or remain in silence. Trust your God source t guide you. Do the same for yourself as you notice the moments when yo are dumping or processing.

Closing a Session
Setting Boundaries For Future Sessions

Learning to close a session compassionately is just as important as creating a nurturing and safe environment when you open one. stablishing clear boundaries in a loving way early on will help protect our energy levels and create respect for your time and the agreed-upon ngth of your session.

When the client stops asking questions and the reading feels like it is nished, it is important to signify the close of the session. This can be done y asking: "Do you feel complete with the information you have been given day?" Posing this question shows your client that you care about the space at you are holding for her/him and that you are bringing it to a respectful ose. (This is also helpful if you are hired for an event and are limited to ending ten minutes with each person.)

Let's say that you are working with a client who has booked a thirty-inute session with you. When you notice that the time for the person's ssion is almost finished, gently let the person know that s/he has a few oments left, and ask if the client has one or two last questions to ask. This quiry allows you to compassionately signal to the client that it is time to ring the session to a close.

Sometimes you will get a client who has "one last question" and that "question" lasts for four or more questions. It is appropriate at that time let the client know that the initial thirty minutes is finished and that you will happily end with that question or extend the session. If you do not have the time to extend the session, you can offer to book another session with that person at a later date.

When the client has indicated that s/he feels complete with the information you have provided, give her/him a three-to-four sentence summary of their reading. Summarize the current themes that appear in the story. Creating clarity, giving support, and offering hope are the gifts we offer as readers. These are our tools when working with clients who are "dumpers" or "processors." When the individual leaves feeling empowered and heard, we have done our job. This is how we facilitate healing with our words.

Think about different ways that you can bring your sessions to a close and some boundaries that you would like to set early on in your practice. These could include:

- Clients running late
- Clients forgetting an appointment
- When and how clients will compensate you for your services
- How many "one last questions" you will allow
- Whether or not the client can record the session
- Whether or not other friends/family members can be present
- Whether or not two people can share a session

This is only a sample of possible scenarios. The ability to create clear boundaries with a client shows that you are professional and that you value both the client's time and your own. If you choose not to establish boundaries and later become upset because either you or your time is not being respected, the only person you can hold accountable for that situation is yourself. Besides, that kind of energy will only cloud the reading and block your connection with the Divine. Do you see how establishing clear boundaries in a loving way is a crucial part of creating a safe, nurturing environment for both you and your client?

Healthy Aftercare for Your Client

As readers, we need to be aware of our own limits and support people within the scope of our expertise. Remember that there are only two authors of your clients' stories: them and their God source. Sometimes, our ego has the need to try and be more then we truly need to be for our client. If you find yourself becoming too involved in another person's story, take a moment, and honestly ask yourself: Why? Ask for the lesson behind it, and move on.

Instead, know your scope of expertise and create a list of sources to which you could refer them. This ensures healthy aftercare for your clients and is also a great way to cross-network with and support other practitioners. You may already have a list, which will grow with your practice. Keep this list on your computer and continue adding to it.

This list may include:

- Life Coaches
- Massage Therapists
- Other Energy Workers (Reiki Practitioners, Past Life Regression Therapists, Shamans, etc.)
- Psychologists
- Psychiatrists
- Acupuncturists
- Chiropractors
- Doctors
- Nutritionists
- Personal Trainers
- Business Coaches
- Social Service Agencies (Legal Aid, Welfare Community Service Organizations, etc.)
- Police/Fire Departments

Take some time today to put together a referral list for your future clients.

DAY 86

Clearing Yourself and Your Deck

Clearing is one of the most easily forgotten yet key parts of the reading. If you forget to clear yourself after a reading, the energetic cord that was created between you and your client remains intact. While it is important to be connected during the time span of the reading, it is essential for the connection to close when you are finished. Clearing the energy signals the Divine that the "me" part of you is ready to return. When you forget to clear yourself, you could experience energy drainage, a headache, or an ungrounded feeling.

Clearing can be done in a variety of ways and depends on personal preference. Some possibilities for clearing are: a closing/clearing prayer, visualization, breath-work, bathing/showering or physical movement (yoga or cardiovascular exercise). See the below prayer as a suggestion:

Prayer for Closing and Clearing:

Masters, teachers, and guides, thank you for the messages that passed through me for (insert name here). As I close this session, please infuse any lingering energy with love and light and return it to God. Allow these next three breaths I take to clear and ground me as I go about the rest of my day filled with your Divine love and grace.

* If you are going to give consecutive readings use the following version

Masters, teachers, and guides, thank you for the messages that passed through me for (insert name here). As I close this session please infuse any lingering energy with love and light and return it to God. Allow these next three breaths I take to clear and ground me as I continue to be a clear channel of unconditional love for the next person for whom I am about to give a reading.

My favorite method is cleansing with water. After a reading, I usual drink a good amount of water and hop in the shower. Sometimes, as th water hits me, I imagine all of the leftover, unwanted energy washing dow the drain. I also enjoy spending a few moments doing a yoga stretch cardiovascular exercise. If you are familiar with yoga, doing the "breath fire" for three-to-five minutes works well. The heat created in your syste helps to burn away energy that is left after the reading.

Clearing Yourself
While Giving Readings at an Event

When you give readings at an event and want to clear energy betwee each client, you can shuffle the cards in between and imagine the energ from each client leaving as that person walks away. Then, as the next persc sits down and shuffles, imagine the deck is now infused with that person energy. I place a clear crystal (quartz or selenite) on the deck or on the tabl when I am giving readings at an event. This helps to cleanse the space fc me. I also hold a crystal in my hands in between working with each clien

Another way to cleanse is to stay hydrated with fresh water. As yo drink, envision the water clearing away any unwanted energy. At som point during an event, try getting up and going to the restroom: wash you hands, and do some breath-work. Remember, clearing yourself and you environment is important to ground yourself and create a sense of clarity

Make a list of ten different ways
that you could clear yourself after giving a reading:

1.

2.

3.

4.

5.

6.

7.

8.

9.

0.

Storing and Clearing Your Deck

As you decide how to store your deck, choose a method that works for you. Some people like cloth pouches, while others prefer boxes. I use a wooden box that my teacher gave me when I first started reading Tarot. Years later, I was given a beautiful mini clear quartz crystal that I keep inside the wooden box to hold the cards. When my cards are at home, a larger piece of clear quartz rests on top of the box. I use clear quartz and selenite to cleanse my deck. Some of my friends burn sage to cleanse their cards after each use. Do whatever feels right to you.

How will you store your deck?

Finish the following sentence: I clear my deck by:

DAY 87

The Ten Steps to Giving a Reading

Now, let's put all of these pieces together and look at the TEN steps involved in giving a reading.

Do a grounding exercise (meditation or breath-work).
Connect with your client and create a safe space.
Say a Prayer of Intention.
Lay out the initial Celtic Cross and begin sharing.
Practice the *Five-Second Drill* as you intuitively lay cards over
the initial Celtic Cross and go through the entire deck.
Give the client the opportunity to ask questions.
Continually practice the *Making a Person Your Meditation* exercise.
Ask the client if s/he feels complete with the information
that has been shared before you close the session.
Give a three-to-four-sentence summary of the themes present in the reading.
After the client leaves, clear the energy created by the reading.

Do another reading for yourself today. Practice by looking back at the templates from **Day 81 or Day 82** and, this time, try to complete the reading without writing anything down. Record the session so that you can just let go and allow the messages come through you as you speak them aloud. After you are done, listen to the recording and enjoy.

DAY 88

Respecting People's Boundaries

Years ago, I entered into a roommate situation with four other people, and I developed a bond of sisterhood with Rachel, one of the women, her quickly. One night as we talked, she admitted that she had been a tle afraid to become friends with me. When I asked her why, she said that e was nervous that I would always be reading her and know what she as thinking. This was not the first time I had heard this from the people my life.

The truth is that if I spent all of my time reading people, I would exhausted. Let me also add that I find reading people without their rmission to be rude and intrusive. The times when I receive messages d share them are the times I have been asked to give a reading. If I am not ving a reading and I receive messages about someone, I ask the person's rmission to share that information first. I usually say something like: "I n getting some information about what you are going through; would u like me to share it with you?" If the person says yes, I do. If the person ys no, I don't.

A person's story is his or her own. That person will decide if and when look for insight. I have been around other intuitive readers, psychics, or ediums, and I don't like it when someone starts telling me messages s/he receiving about me without asking me if I want hear the information first. As you e developing your intuition, it is tural that there will be times hen you receive messages out people around you ithout them asking u to tap in.

The bottom line:

LWAYS ASK ERMISSION) SHARE THE IFORMATION)U ARE ECEIVING.

Respect the rights of others to choose.

When people choose to receive the messages, it means that they a
receptive to looking deeper at the stories they are creating in their own live
Sharing without permission could throw an unreceptive person furth
into the story because the person feels a need to protect her/his theme. T
people who are receptive to the messages are the ones who ask you for
reading or give you permission to share.

Today is the day for you to give a reading to another person. Ask you
friends or family members if they would like to receive a reading. T
reading can be done in person, on the phone, or via the internet (Skyp
FaceTime, etc., are good tools). You can look back at the templates fro
Day 81 or Day 82 to review if you would like. As you have already don
try giving the reading by just speaking it as you lay the cards down. As yo
connect to the Divine and allow the messages to flow through you, they wi

DAY 89

How Often
Should One Get a Reading?

A nother commonly asked question is about how often one should get a reading. This answer is unique for each person asking the question. My response when a client asks me how often they should return is this: "Trust yourself; you will know when it is time. When you wonder whether or not it is time for a reading, sit quietly with that for a day or two. When you get a definite feeling of, 'Yes, this is time,' call me for an appointment." Encourage the person's power of choice.

Monday	Tuesday	Wednesday	Thursday	Friday
1	2	3	4	5
8	9	10	11	12
15	16	17	18	19
22	23	24	25	26
29	30	31		

Once, when I was interviewed by a psychic hotline, I was encouraged to talk slower and form bonds with phone clients so that they would become "repeat weekly or daily clients." Encouraging dependency and drawing out my answers (because I speak quickly) when sharing information were two things that went against my beliefs. Needless to say, all parties involved decided that it would not be a good fit for me to work there.

Your intention when giving a reading is to help someone get back to believing in themselves and connecting within. If you are interested in creating a relationship that consists of clients who cannot make a decision without consulting you, this book is not for you.

Some of my clients receive a reading every few months and some, once or twice per year. When they are looking for anything sooner than that, I suggest that they consider a session of Life Coaching. Generally, not a lot changes in the period of a month. Allowing a client to get into the habit of frequent readings is creating a co-dependent relationship, while the Life Coaching approach creates an opportunity for your clients to re-learn to trust their own choices.

260 HOWOFTENSHOULDONEGETAREADING?

Also, if clients are serious about creating lasting changes quickly and want more frequent contact, the life-coaching relationship offers support in a healthy way. It reinforces their ability to make choices while creating accountability for their actions. Perhaps you yourself are also a life coach or you know of a good one. You can offer your services as a life coach after the reading or recommend someone that you know. A life coach is great when people are looking for frequent "check-in's" and wish to create accountability because they are ready to dive into changing their theme.

People may also be ready to change their themes on their own and incorporate their own practices to connect to the Divine Storyteller on a more regular basis. If they choose this, support their choice by encouraging them and asking them what they are committed to changing before they leave.

Today, try giving another reading to yourself or someone else.

Gratitude

Dear Reader,

Wow! You have traveled so far since Day 1. During the first part of your journey, you learned to know yourself better as you took an honest look at your patterns and habits. You also learned the importance of the breath and started exploring the concept of themes and stories within your life and the life of your clients. Finally, you connected with your intuition. In Part Two you connected with your deck and spent some time with each card. Finally, you learned how to put all of that knowledge together and give a reading in Part Three.

I understand that there will be ups and downs, because I have experienced them myself and continue to during my journey. What I have come to realize is that when my misery is stronger than my joy, it means that my big fat ego has gotten in the way. Sometimes, I forget that Divine support is always available and withdraw from my God source with the belief that I could do it all on my own.

Although you have finished the lessons, your journey is just beginnin
Hopefully you have discovered some new, juicy information about yoursel
I know that your intuition and ability to connect to your God source ha
really opened up. Continue to enjoy the experiences granted to you b
each reading. Remember, giving a reading is NOT about memorizing th
meanings of the cards or being right or wrong. Giving a reading is abou
connecting, letting go and allowing flow.

May you move past your own outdated themes and stories effortlessl
and easily. Your own story is now well on the way to becoming a bestselle
When in doubt, take a deep breath and put God back in the driver's sea
You are never alone.

Since beginning my journey, I have consumed many books in my searc
for God. I laugh as I write this because, truly, all it takes is surrendering an
allowing oneself to connect to the Divine. Along my path, several book
helped to remind me of that and also shared key information that I neede
in order to navigate successfully as a human in this world. Below is a li:
of the resources I found highly supportive and that you might like to loo
into on this final day of your journey:

- *Non-Violent Communication* by Marshall B. Rosenberg
- *A Course In Miracles* by The Foundation for Inner Peace
- *The Gifts of Imperfection* by Brené Brown
- *Proof of Heaven: A Neurosurgeon's Journey Into the Afterlife*
  by Eben Alexander
- *Secrets of Meditation: A Practical Guide to Inner Peace
  and Personal Transformation* by Davidji
- *Ayurveda: The Science of Self-Healing* by Dr. Vasant Lad
- *Chakra Yoga: Balancing Energy for Physical, Spiritual,
  and Mental Well-Being* by Alan Finger with Katrina Repka
- *The Artist's Way* by Julia Cameron
- *A New Earth* by Eckhart Tolle

May you always remember that your purpose when giving readings i
to remind your clients of their dreams and possibilities, to reconnect ther
with their God source, and to give them an experience of unconditiona
love. You are choosing to be a conduit for the Divine to help loosen an
constrictions others may be experiencing in their own lives.

As a reader, it is your purpose to share your clients' current themes with them and offer messages that help them live a bestselling life. Supporting their reconnection with the Divine, their God source, while staying connected with yours, is what it is all about. The world will become an even better place because of the work that you are about to embark upon and all of the love that you are about to share. This is the true path to living "happily ever after" and healing with your words.

If you have any questions, feel free to reach out to me at readingswithlorri@yahoo.com. Also, if you would like to share, I would love to hear about how this experience has transformed your life. Thank you for taking this journey with me.

With Love & Gratitude,

Lorri

Appendix

CONSCIOUS BREATHING
(FROM DAY 2)

Part 1.
Connecting to Your Body

1. Allow yourself to sit up straight and tall.

2. Close your eyes and take a deep breath in through your nose, an then exhale through your nose. Become aware of the expansion the occurs as you inhale.

3. As you take in oxygen, feel your muscles expand and your spir extend up toward the ceiling. Be aware of the muscular contraction that occur with every exhalation.

4. As you expel oxygen, feel your muscles contract or hug closer int your bones. Feel the spaces between the discs in your spine becom smaller.

5. Close your eyes and breathe like this for a total of ten deep breath Practice being aware of the difference you feel in your muscles whe you inhale and exhale. Sink into the experience.

art 2.
onnecting to Your Intuition

Next, allow yourself to inhale for as long as you can. (Inhale to the point here you cannot take in any more air.) Hold that breath for as long as you n, until it becomes uncomfortable.

Now, exhale the breath slowly for as long as possible. When you have ached the end of your exhalation, hold your breath for as long as you can.

Do this for three more cycles and then stop.

art 3.
reating Balance In Your Body, Mind, & Spirit

Try the exercise from Part 2 while you practice each part of the cycle for e same amount of time. Perhaps you can start by being in each part of the ʳcle for four seconds: inhaling for four seconds, holding for four seconds, ᴛhaling for four seconds, and holding for four seconds.

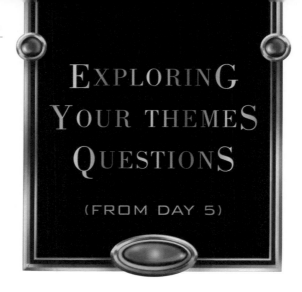

EXPLORING YOUR THEMES QUESTIONS

(FROM DAY 5)

1. Write down a message that your parents (or the adults around you) consistent repeated about loving relationships, work or money.

2. What have you learned from the views of society, your peers, and the mec on this particular subject?

3. What beliefs emerged from the messages that were shared?

4. How do these beliefs affect your current life story?

5. How do these themes support your current life story:

   Physically?
   Emotionally?
   Mentally?
   Spiritually?

6. How do these messages lead to limitations in your life?

7. Are the messages that were shared with you true?

8. What is the new message you would like to share with yourself?

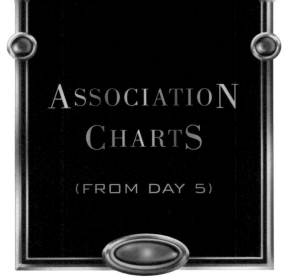

Color	Association
Red	
Orange	
Yellow	
Green	

Blue	
Purple	
White	
Brown	
Black	
Grey	
Gold	
Silver	

Number	Association
Zero (0)	
One (1)	
Two (2)	
Three (3)	
Four (4)	
Five (5)	

Six (6)	
Seven (7)	
Eight (8)	
Nine (9)	
Ten (10)	

Word	Association
Water	
Fire	
Earth	
Air	
King	
Queen	
Knight	
Page	

FIVE-SECOND
DRILL

(FROM DAY 76)

1.   Start by shuffling the deck.

2.   Close your eyes and take three deep breaths while you shuffle.
     This will help you connect with your deck.

3.   When you are ready, stop shuffling, turn over the top card and look at it.

4.   As you look at the card, say the first word that comes to your mind.
     (Remember, there are no right or wrong answers.)
     You may say anything from a color or a number to a random
     thought, noun, verb, name, etc. Whatever comes up is perfect.

5.   Turn over the next card and repeat the actions of number 4.

6.   Continue this pattern until you have gone through each card in your deck.

7.   Move through the deck quickly. If no ideas come through, move to the next
     card, creating a pile of the "blank" cards, so that you can explore them later

Reminder: Only spend five seconds or less on each card

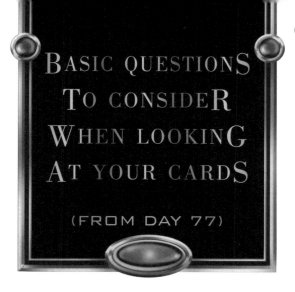

BASIC QUESTIONS
TO CONSIDER
WHEN LOOKING
AT YOUR CARDS

(FROM DAY 77)

1. What colors stand out to you?

2. Do any numbers grab your attention?

3. Do you notice a person or an animal on the card?

4. What action or story is being shown on the card?

What is the overall feeling being represented in the card? Do the actions in the card have a feeling of calmness? Happiness? Sadness? Anger?

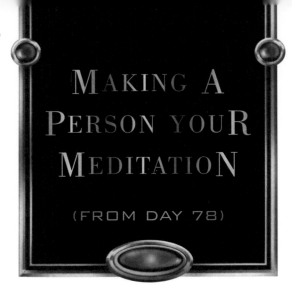

MAKING A PERSON YOUR MEDITATION

(FROM DAY 78)

1. As your friend or family member shares their story with you, give that person your full attention.

2. Focus solely on the person's words.

3. As you inhale and exhale, imagine that you are breathing the words in and ou

4. Engage in soft eye contact (don't stare intently or intensely) with a pleasan warm look on your face.

5. Listen from your heart.

6. As the person speaks, breathe deeply in and out through your nose.

7. Take the breath all the way down to your belly.

8. Breathe this way the entire time the person is sharing.

9. Avoid nodding or making noises of agreement/disagreement while yo partner is speaking, unless s/he stops and waits for a response.

10. When the person asks you for a response, allow the words to flow through yo as you connect with the Divine. Respond from this space with Divine connectio

11. Keep your attention on your partner's words.

12. Allow the words to flow through you like a current flowing through a wire

PRAYER OF INTENTION

(FROM DAY 79)

asters, teachers and guides, allow my ego and I to step aside and be a clear annel to receive and share the messages for (*insert name here*) from her/ s masters, teachers, and guides. I ask that the messages be for the highest d best for all involved all in the name of love. Thank you.

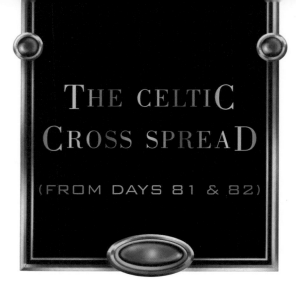

THE CELTIC CROSS SPREAD

(FROM DAYS 81 & 82)

Card One:
The situation that the client currently experiences.

Card Two:
The theme that either helps or hinders the situation.

Card Three:
An event, feeling, thought, or experience that leads to Card Four.

Card Four:
What is being let go of because of Card Three.

Card Five:
A new possibility about to enter one's life.

Card Six:
What may happen as a result of Card Five.

*Card Seven:
The client's current standing or state of mind.

*Card Eight:
The outer environment, people, places, or things that affect the client.

*Card Nine:
Possible hopes and fears of the client.

*Card Ten:
The outcome based on the client's current theme.

Also, try reading cards seven through ten together as a sentence and see what happens.

PRAYER FOR CLOSING AND CLEARING:

(FROM DAY 86)

Masters, teachers, and guides, thank you for the messages that passed through me for (insert name here). As I close this session, please infuse any lingering energy with love and light and return it to God. Allow these next three breaths I take to clear and ground me as I go about the rest of my day filled with your Divine love and grace.

* If you are going to give consecutive readings use the following version:

Masters, teachers, and guides, thank you for the messages that passed through me for (insert name here). As I close this session please infuse any lingering energy with love and light and return it to God. Allow these next three breaths I take to clear and ground me as I continue to be a clear channel of unconditional love for the next person for whom I am about to give a reading.

THE TEN STEPS TO GIVING A READING

(FROM DAY 79)

1. Do a grounding exercise (meditation or breath-work).

2. Connect with your client and create a safe space.

3. Say a Prayer of Intention.

4. Lay out the initial Celtic Cross and begin sharing.

5. Practice the *Five-Second Drill* as you intuitively lay cards over the initial Celtic Cross and go through the entire deck.

6. Give the client the opportunity to ask questions.

7. Continually practice the *Making a Person Your Meditation* exercise.

8. Ask the client if s/he feels complete with the information that has been shared before you close the session.

9. Give a three-to-four-sentence summary of the themes present in the reading.

10. After the client leaves, clear the energy created by the reading.